WITHDRAWN

Performing Arts Resources

Performing Arts Resources

Edited by Ted Perry
With the editorial assistance of Barbara Skluth

VOLUME TWO, 1975

**Drama Book Specialists (Publishers)
Theatre Library Association
New York**

© Copyright 1976 by Theatre Library Association

First Edition

All rights reserved

No part of this publication may be reproduced or transmitted in any form or by any means, electronic or mechanical, including photocopy, recording, or any information storage and retrieval system now known or to be invented, without permission in writing from the publishers, except by a reviewer who wishes to quote brief passages in connection with a review written for inclusion in a magazine, newspaper or broadcast.

All rights reserved under the International and Pan American Copyright Conventions. For information address Drama Book Specialists (Publishers), 150 West 52nd Street, New York, N.Y. 10019.

Library of Congress Cataloging in Publication Data
Perry, Ted
  Performing Arts Resources
  1. Performing arts—Library resources—United States—Periodicals. I. Theatre Library Association.
Z6935.P46   016.7902'08   75-646287
ISBN 910482-73-X

Printed in the United States of America

Table of Contents

Foreword vii
Preface ix
Notes on Contributors xi

Eileen Bowser
Guidelines for Describing Unpublished Script Materials 1

Mary C. Henderson
With the Compliments of The Raymond Mander & Joe Mitchenson Theatre Collection 9

Joel Zuker
Ralph Sargent's *Preserving the Moving Image*: A Summary Review 15

James E. Fletcher and W. Worth McDougald
The Peabody Collection of the University of Georgia 31

Mark S. Auburn
Promptscripts of *The Rivals*: An Annotated Bibliography 41

Richard Dyer MacCann
Reference Works for Film Study 57

David Haynes
A Descriptive Catalogue of the Filmic Items in the Gernsheim Collection 69

Foreword

The major function of a theatre library is to provide the resources from which the scholar can construct his analyses of past or present. That these resources for theatre research are widely scattered and underpublicized makes the scholar's task more difficult.

It is toward the solution of this problem that the Theatre Library Association directs its annual volume, *Performing Arts Resources*. We hope that the discussion of the contents and locations of theatre collections, both public and private, will result in easier accessibility and higher standards of scholarship.

The contents of this annual will demonstrate the concern of the Theatre Library Association with the entire field of the performing arts, excepting only dance and music which are well represented in other journals.

If you are making your first acquaintance with TLA through this annual, you are invited to become a member and to become a contributor to future annuals.

Robert M. Henderson
President
Theatre Library Association

Preface

Attempting to provide documentation for theatre, film, television and popular entertainments, each annual volume of *Performing Arts Resources* includes articles on storage and use of non-print resources, studies of curatorship, indexes, bibliographies, subject matter guides to various archives and collections, analyses of individual collections and museums, descriptions of regional holdings in a particular field or subject matter, and thorough surveys of research materials, government holdings and training programs in the performing arts. While the major portion of each annual volume of *Performing Arts Resources* is devoted to describing and indexing resources for research, some articles treat such issues as historiography, methodology and states of research in the performing arts.

Each annual volume of *Performing Arts Resources* is envisioned then as a collection of articles which will enable the performing arts student, scholar and archivist to locate, identify and classify information about theatre, film, broadcasting and popular entertainments.

Manuscripts for future volumes of *Performing Arts Resources* should be submitted, along with self-addressed envelopes, to the editor at the Theatre Library Association, 111 Amsterdam Avenue, New York, New York, 10023. Subscription orders should be sent to the same address.

Notes on Contributors

EILEEN BOWSER is the Associate Curator, Department of Film, Museum of Modern Art in New York City, and the President of the Documentation Commission, Federation Internationale des Archives du Film (FIAF).

MARY C. HENDERSON has been a teacher of theatre for many years. She has written a book, *The City and the Theatre*, and a number of articles which have led her to seek out theatre collections wherever she can find them.

JOEL ZUKER is a doctoral candidate, Department of Cinema Studies, New York University, and an Instructor in the Department of Theatre and Cinema, Hunter College, City University of New York.

JAMES E. FLETCHER is an Assistant Professor at the Henry W. Grady School of Journalism, the University of Georgia. Articles by him on broadcasting subjects have appeared in numerous journals. W. WORTH McDOUGALD is Professor and Head, Radio-Television-Film, in the same journalism school. He has been associated with the George Foster Peabody Awards since 1949 and currently serves as Director.

MARK S. AUBURN is Assistant Professor in the Department of English, Ohio State University.

RICHARD DYER MacCANN is the author of numerous articles and books on the cinema, editor of *Cinema Journal*, and Professor of Cinema in the broadcasting-film division at the University of Iowa.

DAVID HAYNES is an Audio Visual Educational Specialist at the Institute of Texan Cultures, University of Texas at San Antonio.

Eileen Bowser

Guidelines for Describing Unpublished Script Materials[1]

The *Guidelines for Describing Unpublished Script Materials* were issued in 1974 as a recommendation of the Documentation Commission of the Federation Internationale des Archives du Film (FIAF) to member archives. This was a preliminary step toward a proposed international listing of script holdings in the archives. As no archive has yet completed cataloguing their holdings according to the Guidelines, and only two archives have begun to do so, it may be anticipated that such an international catalogue is still many years in the future. If any institution, whether or not a member of FIAF, should decide to adopt these Guidelines, the Documentation Commission would be interested to know about it. We would welcome any comments about problems encountered in applying them, in order that we may consider them for future revisions.

FIAF established the Documentation Commission in 1968 at its London Congress, to coordinate documentation efforts in film archives all over the world. The major achievement of the Commission has been to establish the *International Index to Film Periodicals*, which has been in existence since January 1972. It is a collaborative effort of documentation experts in 24 film archives, now indexing 80 internationally recognized film journals, with annotations in English. The *Index* provides a continuously up-to-date card service by subscription for libraries. It is also cumulated and published in annual volumes.

The Federation Internationale des Archives du Film was founded in 1938, to promote the preservation of the film as art and historical document and to bring together all organizations devoted to this end; to facilitate the collection and international exchange of films and documents relating to the cinematographic history and art, for the purpose of making them as widely accessible as possible; to develop cooperation between its members; and to promote the development of cinema art and culture. Today, there are 42 member archives in FIAF, representing over 30 countries. To forward its aims, FIAF has established working commissions for preservation, cataloguing, documentation and copyright problems. The Preservation Commission has published a manual on film preservation, and has in preparation further chapters on the preservation of color film and videotape. The Cataloguing Commission has in preparation a manual on the principles of archival film cataloguing.

Guidelines for Describing Unpublished Script Materials

These guidelines are prepared for international use in the exchange of information about unpublished script materials held by film archives or other institutions. They might also be applied to a catalogue of scripts designed for internal use, but there is a special need for a standard way of describing materials for which we have no common terminology from country to country. Indeed, the terms traditionally used to describe scripts vary from one studio to another and from one time period to another, even within the same country. We have attempted to find categories that would be based on an examination of the materials to be catalogued, rather than a system requiring a thorough knowledge of film production methods.

The word "script" is used here in the broadest sense, and is meant to include the many different stages of preparation in film production, from the merest outline of a story or an idea to the most detailed record of the completed film.

There are two kinds of information to be recorded, which should be clearly separated from each other by a space. The first serves to identify the film, the second describes the script materials. The list, or the cards, should be arranged in alphabetical order of the film title, disregarding articles.

THE FILM. The format in use for the FIAF *International Index to Film Periodicals* is followed here:

The original title of the film in country of origin is followed in parentheses by the abbreviation for country of origin, the name of the director, and the year of first public showing. Example:

BEST YEARS OF OUR LIVES, THE (US, William Wyler, 1946)

If the original title is not known, the alternate title should be placed inside brackets. The standard abbreviations for country may be found in the *International Index to Film Periodicals*.

THE SCRIPT. The details which follow should appear in the order given here:

1. **Script category.** There are four main categories, indicated by Roman numerals, as defined below. The word "Script" precedes the Roman numeral, to make it clear that script materials are being described, and the kind of category should be underlined to make it stand out in the body of the text.

   These categories attempt to follow the logic of production, i.e., pre-production, production and post-production materials, but these terms are difficult to define and may overlap. The category number should be followed, *always* in quotation marks, by the term which is found on the materials, e.g., "scenario," "shooting script," "second revision," "final shooting script," "dialogue cutting continuity," "dialogue sheets" or any terms used, in the language in which they appear, exactly as they occur. If no such terms appear on the materials, the script category should stand alone.

Definitions:

Script I indicates or describes the action, but does not break the action into separate shots.

Script II does break the action into separate shots, but does not indicate the length of the shots.

Script III does indicate the length of each shot.

Script IV contains only the dialogue or intertitles and does not describe the action. Note that *Scripts I, II* and *III* may or may not include dialogue or intertitles, but must describe the action.

Note: Even with definitions as precise as the above, there will be some scripts which combine elements of each. In that case, the decision as to category should be made on the basis of the elements which predominate.

2. **Title.** Use only if the title on the script differs from the film title. The script title should appear in lower case letters, the film title in upper case letters.

3. **Authors.** Use only if on the script materials, employing the same terms as on the materials, in the language in which they appear. Do not use information from other sources, as it frequently differs from that given on the script.

4. **Date.** Use only if found on the script. The date should be written in international style, e.g., 15 Feb 1915. If later pages of revisions have been inserted, the date should be followed by "+ revisions," e.g., 8 Mar 1948 + revisions. This will indicate that the actual date is later than the date given, but avoids the necessity of examining all inserted pages to determine the latest date. If the only

dates to be found on the script are on the revised pages, the latest date may be used.

5. **Pages.** The number followed by p. If pages are not numbered, they should be approximated, e.g., ca 250 p.

6. **Notes.** Give here any other descriptive information or qualifying remarks not covered by the guidelines. For example, should the script be written in a language which is not the same used by the country of origin of the film, it should be noted here. Should the script contain handwritten notations, or include a shooting schedule, or any additional material, this is the place to note these facts.

7. If the catalogue of unpublished scripts is intended for external use, the name of the institution holding the script must appear. If the script is available for interlibrary loan, that fact should be noted. It should be remembered that unpublished scripts are usually the property of the producing company, and no copying or publication may be permitted without the consent of the owner of the rights.

There will be some scripts for films which were never made. They present special problems because one cannot catalogue them by title of the completed film. The guidelines set forth here do not apply to them. It is recommended to catalogue them separately, by author, under the heading SCRIPTS, UNREALIZED.

For some specific applications of the guidelines, see the following examples:

>BEST YEARS OF OUR LIVES, THE (US, William Wyler, 1946)
>*Script II.* 9 Apr 1946 + revisions. 220 p.
>Available for interlibrary loan.

BLOCKADE (US, William Dieterle, 1938)
Script II, "final continuity." The river is blue, by John Howard Lawson. 28 Feb 1938. 126 p.

BUDENJE PACOVA (YU, Živojin Pavlović, ca 1964)
Script I, "résumé du sujet." 1 p. in French.
Script II, "liste des dialogues." By Dragoljub Ivkov. 35 p. in French.
Above scripts are bound together.

BOTTOMLESS PIT, THE (US, Scott Sidney, 1915)
Script II. Scenario by William H. Clifford and Thomas H. Ince. ca 25 p. Handwritten notations throughout. Contains shooting schedule and list of locations. Edges burned by fire.

CROSSFIRE (US, Edward Dmytryk, 1947)
Script II, "final script." Cradle of fear, by John Paxton, based on the novel, The brick foxhole, by Richard Brooks. 19 Feb 1947 + revisions. 102 p.
Script III. Screenplay by John Paxton, adapted from a novel by Richard Brooks. ca 75 p.

CASO DOS IRMÃOS NAVES, O (BL, Luis Sergio Person, 1967)
Script IV, "lista de dialogos." 68 p. in English.

CHINMOKU (JA, Masahiro Shinoda, 1972)
Script II. Silence, adapted by Shusaku Endo and Masahiro Shinoda from the novel by Shusaku Endo. 128 p. in English and Japanese.

BROKEN DREAMS (US, Robert Vignola, 1933)
Script III, "list of superimposing instructions." Screenplay by Maude Fulton. 15 Nov 1933. 31 p.
Script IV, "dialogue script." 24 p. Contains handwritten notations.
Script IV. 10 p.
Script IV. 12 p. in Portuguese.
Script IV, "list of Spanish superimposed titles." 18 Nov 1933. 22 p. in Spanish.
Above scripts are bound together.

BLOOD ON THE ARROW (US, Sidney Salkow, 1964)

Script IV, "dialogue continuity" and "spotting list." Screenplay by Robert R. Kent, based on a story by Robert R. Kent and Mark Hanna. 1964. 69 p.

POPIÓL I DIAMENT (PL, Andrzej Wajda, 1958)
Script III, "post-production shooting script." Screenplay by Jerzy Andrzejewski and Andrzej Wajda, based on the novel by Jerzy Andrzejewski. 141 p. in English.

PUGAČEV (UR, P. Petrov-Bitov, 1937)
Script II, "montaznka list." Po scenario Olga Forš. 1937. 78 p.
Script IV. 34 p.
Script IV, "dialogue." 22 p. in English.
Script IV, "dialogue." Pugachev, The days of Catherine the Great. Story by Olga Forsh. 24 p. in English. Handwritten notations. Corrected for censors.
Above scripts are bound together.

CHAIN LIGHTNING (US, Lambert Hillyer, 1927)
Script II, "continuity." By Lambert Hillyer. ca 60 p.

Notes

1. Copyright 1974, International Federation of Film Archives (FIAF), 74 Galerie Ravenstein, 1000 Brussels, Belgium. Reprinted with permission. Prepared by the Documentation Commission of FIAF. First edition. Information about FIAF and its publications may be obtained from the Secretariat at the address above.

Mary C. Henderson

With the Compliments of The Raymond Mander & Joe Mitchenson Theatre Collection

One of the great theatre collections in the English-speaking world reposes not in some glass or marble edifice but in a three-story row house in Sydenham, a workingclass suburb of London. What immediately sets this particular house apart from its red-brick neighbors is that it looks neater and trimmer in its mauve-gray painted exterior than the rest of the block. Another telltale sign of its latent distinction is the bust of Shakespeare peering out of the front window. No. 5 Venner Road, along with the rest of the houses in the row, was rescued from demolition by a government agency not long ago, and the massive job of relocating the treasures contained within its walls has been postponed to a more auspicious time.

The house belongs to Joe Mitchenson, who with Raymond Mander resides both with and for their mutually acquired and shared theatre collection. The collection fills both the upper stories and the basement and is a part of their living and working quarters. Surprisingly, everything fits in so well with the personalities of the tenants and their familial antique furnishings that it looks not at all like a museum but the proper milieu for their life and work. The future may well change all that. Mander and Mitchenson have proleptically bequeathed their priceless collection to the nation. Together with the William Archer Library, their store of theatrical memorabilia is slated to form the foundation of the National Theatre Museum, which will be housed in the National Theatre, which may someday open its doors on the South Bank of the Thames. Eventually, smaller collections will migrate to the new theatre complex, but how the museum will be arranged, the space it is to be given and the precise function of Messrs. Mander and Mitchenson are yet to be worked out. It is thought, however, that the Enthoven Collection and the British Theatre Museum will remain at their present sites.

It is not easy to describe or catalogue the Mander-Mitchenson collection. In Mr. Mander's own words: "We are rather difficult to convey." But it soon becomes quite evident that the backgrounds and predilections of both partners have given a unique stamp to the collection. Joe Mitchenson comes from a stage family. His father was a drama critic and his grandparents and other assorted relatives were performers. Raymond Mander's family includes architects on the paternal side and engravers on the maternal side. He grew up surrounded by antiques, paintings and scrapbooks and became a precocious collector himself.

The fusion of the two mentalities has resulted in an eclectic, rather eccentric, mountain of theatrical materials that embraces both the usual and the unexpected. Both men have been gifted with an antiquarian's nose for sniffing out the rare or unusual and the historian's zeal for authenticating everything before it joins the august company.

Both men started out to be actors. When their paths crossed in 1939, they discovered their mutual hobby and joined forces to create a mutual obsession. The war did not impede or dampen their fervor for searching and collecting. Despite the difficult times and the fact that Mr. Mitchenson was serving in the armed forces while Mr. Mander was building morale with his programs on BBC radio, they used what spare time they had in ferreting out theatrical antiques. When the two actors trouped the country from 1943 to 1946, they sought out antique shops wherever they were playing. They began their collection of Staffordshire theatrical china in those years, shipping hundreds of pieces back to London in the middle of the war. Inadvertently, they were probably responsible for the preservation of much memorabilia that might well have been lost.

They left the theatre in 1947 to devote all of their time to the collection. They never consciously thought that they were in the process of assembling a museum; they simply considered their purpose as custodial: preserving the past for use in the present. As testament to that fact, they have supplied theatrical iconography for over five hundred books on the theatre and for countless exhibitions, as well as for LP record covers, TV programs and filmed documentaries. They have served as consultants for movies, and their files have yielded information for theatre programs, books, theses, dissertations and articles. They will attempt to answer all reasonable queries "with the compliments of" the Mander and Mitchenson collection. They have even listed themselves in the Yellow Pages under "Theatrical Supplies." Additionally, they have published sixteen books on the British theatre and are working on the seventeenth, all of which contain material from their personal "archives" which has never been in print.

A large part of the collection consists of theatrical documentation from the seventeenth century onward. There are books, theatrical programs, posters and files of stage periodicals. More important than these, the collection contains original promptbooks, some with marginal comments written in by the playwrights, and manuscripts of melodramas used by the Victorian Fit-up Companies. Then, there are manuscript letters and diaries, among which is a piece of a William Charles Macready diary covering his 1844 trip to America. (What makes the latter such a treasure is the fact that all of the Macready diaries were thought to have been destroyed by his son, who did not want his father's frequently uncomplimentary allusions to his contemporaries exposed to public eye.) American scholars looking for clues in Macready's character to explain the tragic events which took place later in the Astor Place Opera House riot could probably find some help in this fragment.

Mander and Mitchenson were presented with the archives of such famous stage families as the Terrys and the Broughs as well as documents from Constance Collier, Samuel Cowell, Sir John Martin-Harvey and, more recently, from John Gielgud, Sybil Thorndike and Edith Evans. Since the partners enjoy a warm personal relationship with most of the theatrical community in Britain, they can probably expect to receive similar gifts in the future from their contemporaries.

But their collection does not end with the printed or handwritten word. It contains relics, stage properties and costumes, from the seventeenth century to the present. Among its treasures are a medallion worn by John Philip Kemble as Hamlet and the pennant carried in David Garrick's funeral procession. Mander and Mitchenson own a sizeable collection of costumes, including many of Henry Irving's for his leading roles. In addition, there are also snuffboxes, matchboxes, trinket boxes and a *pot pourri* of old props, all verified as to authenticity and dated as accurately as possible.

The walls of the house resemble nothing so much as the interior of the Garrick Club in London or the Players in New York. There are paintings and drawings by such theatrical portraitists from the eighteenth and nineteenth centuries as Samuel deWilde, George Clint and John Collier, side by side with designs of settings and costumes from contemporary scenic artists. In their workroom, they have files of photographs of theatrical people, places and things, which are reproduced at a charge as part of their service. The collection also contains memorabilia and material from the sister worlds of the opera, ballet, circus and puppetry.

Perhaps the most interesting part of the Mander-Mitchenson collection is their store of theatrical china and pottery. This includes more than the busts of Shakespeare, Irving, Sir George Robey and other notables scattered liberally around the house, but also the exquisite figurines, vases and pitchers, which they so painstakingly assembled. There are representative pieces from the houses of Derby, Worcester, Staffordshire and Royal Doulton, some of which are now defunct. There is a Staffordshire Jenny Lind and a Bloor Derby Garrick among the over four hundred pieces gracing the tables, dressers and chests around the house. All of it is valuable not because as theatrical china it represents an all but vanished art, but because it frequently provides the historian with a gentle intimation of acting style through the pose of the actor frozen in the figurine. And the costume designer is presented with stage dress in three dimensions.

To their everlasting credit, Mander and Mitchenson have been painstaking preservers and cataloguers of the materials which have passed into their possession. When the day finally arrives that the Mander and Mitchenson collection moves from Sydenham to South Bank, from private collection to public trust, the transition should be effortless, thanks to their prior dedication and solicitude.

Joel Zuker

Ralph Sargent's *Preserving the Moving Image*: A Summary Review

Walter Benjamin, the distinguished literary critic, translator and essayist, wrote an article in 1931 entitled "Unpacking My Library—A Talk About Book Collecting." In the essay, Benjamin characterizes the joys and frustrations of a devout bibliophile. He tells us: "Only in extinction is the collector comprehended." Benjamin's statement is particularly important in terms of this paper because what he says has as much to do with the concept of film preservation as it does with book collecting. Two-thirds of the theatrical films made in this country are lost forever; 163 million feet of nitrate film (approximately 16,000 titles) are in danger of becoming extinct. Therefore, the work of the film conservationist must take on a much greater significance.

Ralph Sargent[1] was commissioned by the Corporation for Public Broadcasting and the National Endowment for the Arts to identify the source of these problems and propose ways to correct them. His efforts are intelligently documented in a book published in 1974 called *Preserving the Moving Image*. More specifically, the study was undertaken to:

1. Determine the ideal archival conditions under which to store film. (Sargent has set forth very specific standards for archival storage covering such factors as Resolution, Gamma Range, Density Range, Color Sensitivity and Stability.)
2. Discover more reliable tests to predict the remaining life of nitrate film.
3. Discover new materials or methods now being developed or that could be developed that would replace the admittedly unsatisfactory procedures as they now exist.
4. Establish priorities for funding more research in those areas that seem most promising.

Sargent's text is organized under six main headings: *Base, Binder, Image; Treatment and Storage; Conditions in the Field; New Approaches; New Technologies;* and *Videotape*. In most cases, I have tried to follow a similar outline in preparing this report.

Base, Binder, Image; Treatment and Storage

Motion picture film consists of three elements: a base, binder and image. Each of these impose certain problems for the archivist. The original base used in the manufacture of motion picture film, cellulose nitrate, is chemically unstable, dimensionally variable, and subject to changes in humidity and temperature. In the preparation of nitrate film,[2] a cellulosic material, such as wood or cotton fiber, is treated with nitric and sulphuric acid. Nitrate and acetate films should never be stored in the same area because the gases that are released by nitrate decomposition can destroy the silver image in an acetate print. Cellulose nitrate contains its own oxidant, has a low point of combustion and once ignited is not easily extinguished. Nitrate will continue to burn when completely submerged in water. It is a highly dangerous substance and should be handled with extreme caution. Many valuable and oftentimes irreplaceable films have been lost in archive fires. In the past twenty years, there have been nitrate explosions at the National Film Board of Canada, the Cinématheque Française and at Bulgaria's Nationala Filmoteka; several people lost their lives. Before World War I, scientists introduced a new base called cellulose diacetate, or "safety film." Poor geometric stability, low tensile strength and lack of flexibility made it unsuitable for professional use. In the 1930s, tests were conducted using a mixed cellulose ester of acetate propionate and acetate butyrate. It was more flexible than diacetate but not strong enough for theatrical use. Cellulose triacetate, developed in the 1940s, was completely esterified, but its limited solubility in conventional solvents prevented its general use. In 1948, a slightly less esterified triacetate, "high acetyl," was made available and soon became the preferred base for theatrical production. Unlike nitrate film, acetate does not exert a harmful influence on other films stored in its immediate vicinity. Polyester or polyethylene teraphthalate was invented by Dupont in 1941. It is an oxygen compound of alcohol and carboxylic acid. Polyester is chemically more stable than either nitrate or acetate. It is so strong that ecologists are concerned about its non biodegradable properties. "Without question, polyester is the best available film base material. It will permit less stringent storage and handling conditions—while at the same time extend the useful life of the film." Polyester shifts the burden of preservation from the base to the image. Some archivists feel that additional testing is needed before polyester can be unconditionally recommended.

The gelatin or "binder" is a transparent protective support for the silver halide crystals in the emulsion. It is an organic product obtained from the partial hydrolysis of collagen from the skins, connective tissues and bones of animals. It is 99.96% pure and contaminated with traces of desirable impurities. It is water permeable and thermally reversible between liquid and solid states. It is not resistant to moisture and can support the growth of damaging fungus. Several products using synthetic substitutes for gelatin have been marketed, but did not prove successful. If proper storage conditions are maintained, the gelatin binder acts as an excellent adhesive substratum.

The preservation of the silver halide image (emulsion) is dependent on correct processing. If poorly "fixed" or improperly washed, the film may become faded or spotted. If carelessly stored, it may be attacked by environmental pollutants. Such deterioration is usually preventable, and where in progress, can be halted and even reversed. Incomplete fixing, residual chemicals or atmospheric oxidants can produce sulfur compounds in the silver images, causing yellowing or fading. Image density decreases and the image may even disappear. If deterioration is not severe, the films may be bleached and redeveloped. Discolored negatives can be regenerated in a solution of iodine and alcohol. The iodine converts yellow silver to silver iodine and the material is then fixed and washed. Black and white images can be restored by a process that uses a strong oxidizing agent and bleaching bath. After washing, the material is immersed in an acidified stannous chloride solution, converting the image silver to halide. It is then rewashed and redeveloped. This procedure can result in a complete regeneration of the image.

Archivists are considering the possible use of "image stripping" as an alternative way of preserving a nitrate print. This involves the removal of the original image layer and its subsequent bonding to a new film base. The original film is conditioned and repitched to standard perforations and temporarily bonded with the emulsion side down to a traveling pinned belt. Solvents are applied to the nitrate base to permit a stripping away of the image layer. After resubbing, the image layer is bonded by heat and compression to a new and stronger base. The bond between the original emulsion and the pinned belt is broken and the film is removed, washed and dried. Another method of image stripping involves essentially the same procedure, except that the original film is bonded to a new base with the emulsion side up. The two bonded films are removed from the pinned belt and placed in a solution that dissolves the old nitrate base but does not disturb the adhesion between the original emulsion layer and the new polyester base. Both approaches are extremely time-consuming and expensive, but the second is probably more satisfactory because fewer steps are required to complete the process.

For the archivist, the treatment and storage of color film constitutes a very special problem. Sargent indicates in his recommendations for Section Two that "even the best specialized storage conditions will do no more than temporarily preserve color dye images." Color films made on an acetate base should be stored on separate black and white negatives—one for each of the three primary colors. This process is expensive and increases the amount of space involved for storage by a factor of three. Also, temperature and humidity must be rigorously maintained between the three negatives, or differential shrinkage and curl rates will prevent reconstitution of the full color image. To preserve the original color material where separations are not practical, the film should be conditioned to between 15 percent and 30 percent relative humidity and stored in sealed containers below zero degrees Fahrenheit. Obviously this kind of optimal situation is impossible to maintain. Humidity control is especially critical. Color films were tested at various levels of humidity at a temperature of 70 degrees for a period of four years. The results indicate deterioration of dyes, particularly cyan, increased at higher moisture levels. Tests documenting the effects of changes in temperature on dye stability, show that they are less stable at higher temperatures.

There are several approaches to color separations;[3] one relies on the creation of three negative images of the primary color information, whether on separate rolls of film or sequentially on one roll. The 70mm Color Separation system proposed by Film Effects of Hollywood, uses standard four sprocket 70mm film, allowing a 1:1 contact printing of the sound track. This format would require only an 18 percent reduction in frame size from 35mm originals, with minimal loss of information. The original can be printed by the "wet-gate" method, exposing the three horizontally parallel primary color frames at once. Full color images would be retrieved by superimposition of the separation images, with the same sort of optical arrangement and color separation filters. In addition to reducing the amount of space required for three separation negatives, this procedure eliminates the possibility of differential rates of shrinkage and distortion, possible loss of one of the separation copies, and inaccurate synchronization in regenerating a positive print.

Another system that can be used separates the color image into a series of analytic units that are encoded by a laser beam onto 35mm film. The angular displacement of these records creates a diffraction grating that later can be separated with spatial filters. RCA superimposes three focused-image holograms, of the separated primary color information, in a single frame using different grating frequencies. Readout is accomplished on a microfilm reader, with white light modified with special optics.

Images can be stored by Electronic Video Recording, or by a combination of optical and electronic techniques. This would permit reconstitution to conventional images and projection on large screens. If the records are made on 35mm film, the scanning pattern may utilize up to twelve hundred lines of information. Experiments conducted by Peter Goldmark, former President and Director of Research at CBS, used Ilford black and white film—a fine grain negative with a gelatin emulsion that is exposed by an electron beam. This procedure requires one-third less storage space than conventional separation systems and may be preferable where image quality can be compromised for projection to small groups. Some archivists believe that color has replaced nitrate as the key issue of film preservation. There is not as yet one definitive solution to the problems. Sargent does state that for color films of acknowledged intrinsic value three strip separations are the only reliable approach presently available. Again the author mandates responsible agencies to provide the necessary funds to conduct additional research in this area.

Conditions in the Field

The next section of *Preserving the Moving Image* is concerned with current conditions in the field. Sargent has provided written transcripts of interviews that he conducted with film archivists in Brussels, London, Rome, Amsterdam and Berlin. Each of the following statements reflects in a particular way some of the serious problems facing film repositories throughout the world:

Jacques Ledoux (Cinématheque Royale de Belgique):

> We are very short of personnel. It is very nice to design a system but you need the people to make it work. We do not even have a catalogue of films ... I think that if you really want to get a picture of the work of an archive, you cannot limit yourself strictly to preservation aspects. This is why I have talked about our side problems—you cannot disconnect them.

Jan de Vaal (Nederlands Filmmuseum):

> A collaborator of ours once phoned me from the technical department to report that he had found a newsreel—Eisenstein visiting Holland in 1929. I was, of course, very enthusiastic and knew we had to do something. He told me not to worry because we had tested it and the results were fine. Because it was such an interesting item, we decided to dupe it anyway. After one year the original was gone completely.

Fausto Montesanti (Cineteca Nazionale):

> I'm an old man. I'm leaving from this world soon. But I'm leaving with my heart in pieces because I can't obtain the necessary funds to dupe everything we have. We have a big collection of Italian silent films, but no money to dupe them.

Wolfgang Klaue (Staatliches Film Archive der D.D.R.):

KLAUE: The problem with storage of color film is that you must have low temperatures and limited humidities (around 30 percent). This creates all kinds of scientific and technical problems.

SARGENT: Given those conditions what will the life expectancy of the films be?

KLAUE: Nobody knows. There was no practical experience until now. There has been some theoretical research done, but nothing practical.

Ernest Lindgren (National Film Archive):

> Under the voluntary system of deposit that we have here, we don't get all that we select or all that we ask for. This is something that we are trying to remedy by acquiring powers of legal deposit such as are already enjoyed by books in the British Museum.

These interviews also serve to correct certain misconceptions regarding the work of a film archivist. He is not merely a custodian of old motion pictures but is usually involved with problems of appraisal, acquisition, funding, exhibition, cataloguing and other ancillary activities.

New Technologies; New Approaches

Section two of the Sargent book examines new techniques for preserving motion picture film. These new advancements will enable the film archivist to preserve and reproduce images with greater efficiency. It will also permit the scholar to study these images in formats incorporating ease of viewing and accessibility at a relatively moderate cost. Sargent proposes three separate archival standards. Archival Medium #1 is for high quality, long-term storage. It will have a resolution of 1200 cycles (line pairs) per horizontal field, and will be the source from which copies can be made. Archival Medium #2 is designed for projection to small groups, such as a classroom situation. Resolution is 600 cycles per horizontal field. Archival Medium #3 is for individual scholarly use. Resolution is 350 cycles per horizontal field. All three categories use materials that have excellent organic properties. Problems such as decomposition, temperature and humidity control, and deficiencies in binder stability are significantly reduced. Many of the systems discussed in this chapter are in various stages of research and cannot at this time be recommended as a replacement for the more traditional methods of recording an image on film. Certainly the most recurrent problem that prohibits the implementation of these new technologies is one of economics. The new systems are not only expensive to produce but in certain cases, such as electro-optical image storage, expensive to maintain.

The Kalvar Corporation in New Orleans has been experimenting with a photographic system which replaces the standard silver halide process with other light sensitive compounds. The theory behind the production of vesicular film images is based upon the shifting or reorganization of microscopic regions of the image layer, resulting in an alteration of the refractive index:

> To illustrate: think of a refractive image as one made up of a multiplicity of prisms, each with a differing geometry. The prisms, representing bright areas of the picture would most closely approach a refractive index of one, whereas the prisms representing darker portions of the picture would have a higher index of refraction. When light is transmitted through this multiplicity of prisms, it is bent and scattered at various angles depending upon the content of the scene.[4]

When Kalvar film is exposed to light certain quantities of nitrogen gas bubbles or vesicles are released. These microscopic bubbles which act as light-scattering centers are trapped within the thermo-plastic matrix of the image layer. Development of the latent image consists of the application of heat to the film, which causes the gas bubbles to expand and permanently deform the matrix of the image. From an archival standpoint, the use of Kalvar film has certain obvious advantages over current procedures:

1. The image produced by vesicular film will not deteriorate for 600 years. (Acetate film or "safety film," if kept in optimal storage conditions, may have a life span of approximately 200 years.)
2. After 2400 passes through a viewer—simulating 150 hours of projection—there was no loss in image quality.
3. The polyester base on which it is manufactured will not tear or rip apart.
4. The durability of vesicular film increases with age. Samples of vesicular film made in 1954 had a thermal resistance of 60% when tested at a temperature of 131 degrees Fahrenheit. When the same film was tested twenty years later under similar conditions of temperature and humidity, the thermal resistance was now 100%.
5. Because the image is not supported by a gelatin layer as it is in silver halide film, the potential growth of fungus is eliminated.

The disadvantages of Kalvar film are:

1. A problem of sensitization to particular colors.
2. Its brightness range is not as great as standard silver grain film.
3. Limited resolution in comparison to other photographic processes.
4. Cost.

Kalvar film is relatively new and its application to archival needs is still highly speculative. In his recommendations at the end of Chapter Two, Sargent strongly supports continued research in this area.

Another information storage system that could be adopted for archival purposes is presented in an interview that Sargent conducted with George Tressel, of Battelle

Memorial Institute in Columbus, Ohio. The Battelle system of digital storage seeks to replace the more traditional method of analogue preservation. The difference between the two systems can be illustrated by setting up a hypothetical problem, concerning the preservation of information contained in a simple folktale. A folktale, by definition, is a story that has been passed down by word of mouth, from generation to generation. Each time the story is told, there is a slight variation in narrative content. After a few generations the original folktale is significantly altered. A comparison can be made to the analogue procedure of producing a "duped print" which is slightly different from the original film. However, an encoding system can be used that will insure the preservation of the original material. In the example of the folktale, an encoding system is achieved by simply writing the story down on a piece of paper. Now that the information contained in the folktale has been converted to a code, i.e., a series of written words, the story can be reproduced without losing any of the original information.

The Battelle system uses a laser beam, a mechanical scanner and computer circuitry to store information in a digital format. The mechanical scanner "searches" the film and breaks the image down into a series of x, y coordinates. The information is recorded as a series of binary dots. The original image can be reconstituted by reversing the process. A light beam is passed over the computer record and a photo-detector picks up the light patterns, converting the image record to an electronic signal. This signal is then transmitted through an ordinary television receiver. The image is rephotographed from a cathode tube.

The specific application of this storage system for archival needs is rather intriguing. In regenerating the original image, one can obtain a high degree of resolution, as in 70mm projection or low resolution, as in videotape. While there is no way of improving the original image, there might be a way in which the system can be used to reconstruct missing segments from a motion picture. Again, let us take a hypothetical situation. A film historian/detective is able to uncover certain information that was used in the production of a particular scene. He would be interested in such factors as production notes, shooting script, camera model, lenses, film stock, weather conditions and so forth. This material could be supplemented by interviews with various technicians who worked on the film. A computer program could be designed which would use all this information in reconstructing the missing segment. A similar procedure has been used by paleontologists in recreating the morphological anatomy of prehistoric animals. The direct application of a digital system, both as a method of preserving film and in the possible restoration of lost footage, is still highly speculative when compared to other available and more proven procedures. As far as the Battelle system is concerned, the breach between theory and *praxis* is still a very real problem. Yet, if this process is ever made operable, the work of the film archivist will take on an entirely new perspective. He will not only be responsible for preserving our film culture but through editorial restoration provide additional materials for study.

Videotape

The last section of the Sargent report is concerned with the technology and preservation of videotape. The author makes it quite clear that our knowledge regarding the archival properties of magnetically recorded images is, at best, cursory. Many questions relating to its adaptibility, to present demands, are still left unanswered:

> Not until recently has the matter of archival storage been seriously considered by the manufacturers of videotape. Not only are age/performance records sloppy, but tests for such performance have not, in many cases, been pursued. . . . Thus those charged with preserving videotapes are doing so "by the seat of their pants," and no confirming test results nor accurate predictions on the long-term keeping qualities of videotape are to be had.[5]

Certainly, one of the most important problems identified in Sargent's introductory comments is the need for greater standardization of existing videotape systems.

> Nearly 100 different models of helical-scan VTR's are presently on the market. Tape widths range from one-quarter inch to two inches. Tape speeds range from 1.26 inches/sec. to 15 inches/sec. Playback times range from 20 minutes to 4,560 minutes (76 hours). There are six different TV standards and four color systems.[6]

When one takes into consideration all the variables suggested here, the problem of preservation becomes one of great complexity. The preservation of motion picture film, in comparison to videotape, seems more manageable. Tests conducted by the National Archives and Records Service "show that approximately 20 percent of a given population of videotape is scrapped each year." This figure is determined by such factors as poor wind, stretching, dust accumulation and deterioration produced by changes in temperature and humidity. Magnetic tape is also highly flammable and the same precautions should be taken in storing videotape as with photographic film.

Sargent indicates that an accurate prediction of the longevity of videotape recordings is between ten and 15 years—a time period which has little or no relevance in archival terms. The temporal quality of magnetic tapes is so restrictive that in many cases they are being converted to 16mm film, in order to guarantee their preservation. Videotape to film transfer can be accomplished by a laser system, an electron beam recording and a kinescope procedure that records directly off the face of the cathode tube during broadcast.

Unlike the problems of photographic film, a specific solution to the inherent difficulties of videotape preservation is not predicated entirely on more funding. Even if further experimentation were conducted, the fact remains that videotape, in its present form, has an abbreviated life span and thus has limited value as a potential source for archival storage. Sargent concludes this section of his report with the following recommendations:

1. It now seems clear that for television originated programming, videotape cannot be relied upon as the master archival medium for permanent storage. Programs chosen to be held for long-term storage must be transferred to film.[7]

2. The best method for accomplishing this—for both black-and-white and color—is to make color separations by means of Electron Beam Recording, because it produces a directly accessible silver image of known archival value.[8]

In one of the scenes of Bertolt Brecht's *Galileo*, there is a discussion between the astronomer and Federzoni, his lens grinder. Galileo says: "The aim of science is not to open the door to everlasting wisdom, but to set a limit to everlasting error." This seems to be the basic task that Sargent has set for himself in writing this book. *Preserving the Moving Image* also seeks to limit everlasting error by establishing clear and cogent guidelines for the scientific conservation of our motion picture heritage. It is unquestionably the definitive study on the subject. All proceeds form the sale of the book will be used by the Corporation of Public Broadcasting and the National Endowment for the Arts to conduct further experimentation with the problems of film and videotape preservation.

Notes

1. Ralph Sargent received his undergraduate training at the University of North Carolina and completed a Master's degree at the University of California at Los Angeles. In 1965-66, he developed, for UCLA, the first high-power, arc-illuminated, 8mm motion picture projector. During 1967-68, while still at UCLA, he invented an automatic exposure control system which, in conjunction with a modified Metro-Kelvar printer, provided completely automatic printing and processing of dry motion picture film. Between 1965 and 1968, he was Production Supervisor for the University of

California Motion Picture Division, and from 1968-71, a Lecturer in the school's film section. He left UCLA in 1971 to form Film Technology Company, Inc. The company offers post-production services and specialized printing for the motion picture industry and for various film archives. Sargent has had experience in both the creative and technical aspects of motion pictures, television and radio.

2. The present procedure for preserving nitrate film is to recopy it onto an acetate base.

3. Many of the procedures discussed in this section are highly theoretical and require additional research.

4. Ralph Sargent, *Preserving the Moving Image*, ed. Glen Fleck (Washington: Corporation of Public Broadcasting and the National Endowment for the Arts, 1974), p. 82.

5. *Ibid.*, p. 131.

6. *Ibid.*

7. *Ibid.*, p. 149.

8. *Ibid.*

James E. Fletcher and
W. Worth McDougald

The Peabody Collection of the University of Georgia

The George Foster Peabody Radio and Television Awards for Distinguished Achievement and Meritorious Public Service have been presented annually since 1941, the awards each year going to programs and program personalities of the previous year. Entries to the Peabody Awards competition are submitted by individual broadcast stations, networks, radio and television editors of newspapers and magazines, listener/viewer groups, and others who wish to direct the attention of the awards to programs they deem of merit. Overall, throughout the history of the awards, the largest numbers of entries have come from stations and networks.

The awards are administered by the Henry W. Grady School of Journalism of the University of Georgia. Currently, Dr. W. Worth McDougald, Head of the Radio-Television-Film Sequence of the Grady School, serves as Director of the Awards. A blue ribbon Advisory Board makes the selections of programs and individuals to receive the Peabody Awards and recommends procedures to be followed in administration of the awards. Mr. Peabody (1852-1938), for whom the awards are named, was a highly successful New York banker who was born in Georgia and who served as a life-trustee of the University of Georgia.

From the beginning, a condition for entry into the annual awards competition has been that no materials submitted with entries can be returned. As a consequence, a relatively large collection of entry materials has accumulated over the past thirty-five years. Today more than 2500 square feet of space are required merely to store these materials. The manifest intent of maintaining these materials has been to provide opportunities for scholars to study the finest programs in American broadcasting and to enlighten the selection process in future Peabody Awards competitions by establishing an enduring perspective upon the content of past American broadcasting. The collection of materials that has accumulated is referred to as the Peabody Collection, although at the time of writing this is an unofficial title.

Unfortunately, the resources available to maintain the Peabody Collection have been extremely limited. In fact, the Collection today is little more than a storage area to which access is strictly limited in order to safeguard the materials. There is no comprehensive catalogue, inventory or index to the materials; there are no facilities with which to make the materials accessible to scholars in a manner that would facilitate research while protecting the materials.

The Peabody Collection is eminently worthy of increased funding to permit its use as a research resource. And with a recent expansion in the Library of the University of Georgia, negotiations are underway to transfer custody of the Peabody Collection to the Library, making the materials accessible for scholarly research.

One unique characteristic of the Peabody Awards is that programs from broadcast groups and local stations as well as networks are considered for and do receive awards. Some recent awards, for example, covering broadcasts of 1973, included *eight* awards to local stations, ranging from such small stations as KANO-FM in Lawrence, Kansas, to such large stations as KNXT, Los Angeles. By contrast *seven* awards went directly to networks. The implications of this practice for the researcher in the Peabody Collection is that he can gain some insight into the relative contribution of local as well as national program output.

The unifying concept of the current effort to bring the Peabody Collection to a state of accessibility which can support and encourage program research, centers around the "Scholar Access Module" (SCAM). The notion of the SCAM implies that the Collection is to serve the needs of scholar users. It is envisioned that interested scholars will apply for or be invited to study in the Collection, occupying a SCAM, a study room equipped with copies of all of the materials of the Collection.

In basic terms three forms of materials have accompanied Peabody entries—papers, audio recordings, video recordings. The papers include entry forms, some scripts, copies of press clippings, reviews, letters from listeners and other explanatory documents. Every entry is represented by at least an entry form or letter. In the tentative planning for the Collection, it is proposed that the papers be reduced to standard four inch by six inch microfiche, with materials for each entry represented by one or two fiche. The convenience, low cost and light weight of microfiche have made it the method of choice for providing copies of all papers in each Scholar Access Module.

Audio recordings initially accompanied about one-third of the radio entries. In the early 1940s the recordings were primarily 16-inch glass transcription discs. By the middle forties, roughly 50 percent of radio entries were accompanied by recordings, and acetate-on-aluminum transcription blanks were in general use. It should be recalled that disc cutting was a relatively expensive and often unsatisfactory recording process as it existed in local stations. The principal use of the transcriptions was to record commercials and frequently used theme music. Several cuts of the same material often had to be made due to the relatively small number of times each cut could be used before a deterioration in sound quality became evident. After World War II the tape recorder came into extensive use in broadcasting, and by the latter 1950s virtually all radio entries to the Peabody Awards were accompanied by tape recordings. Not all recordings are of a single program. A few include excerpts of a variety of programs to illustrate, perhaps, the local news coverage of a station. Other entries, where a program series is proposed for an award, may include recordings of several programs. The exact number of audio recordings surviving in the Peabody Collection will not be known exactly until the materials have been inventoried and catalogued. Some, especially the fragile glass discs of the early 1940s, have been damaged or destroyed. Others may well have been stolen or misplaced. Best, but tentative, estimates of the number of audio recordings indicate that there are more than five thousand in the Collection.

Because of the possibility of unintentional damage to the recordings, the Scholar Access Modules will include audio-cassette copies of the recordings. Audiocassettes were chosen because of low cost, durability and small size. Five thousand audiocassettes in dust-proof containers occupy only about forty-three cubic feet.

The first year for which television entries were received was 1948, when three programs were entered. A Peabody Award that year for "Outstanding Contribution to the Art of Television" went to ABC's "Actors Studio." The earliest television programs in the Collection are copies of films which were broadcast from a television film chain, or 16mm kinescope recording films made from a broadcast program. Videotape began to be used in the late 1950s and today accounts for the majority of television entries to the Peabody Awards. It should be noted that in the early days of television, any capability to record television programs at the local station level were rare. As a result, the television recordings of the Peabody Collection during these years do not include the wealth of local station output present in the radio recordings of the same period. In some cases scripts represent local television station efforts. In a few cases, original 16mm reversal film used on the air in a local telecast was provided with the Peabody entry. As with the radio entries, some video recordings represent excerpts from programs; others include several programs from a series. Best estimates of the number of video recordings in the Collection amount to about four thousand. For the Scholar Access Modules, the film and videotape submitted as entries will be re-recorded on standard three-quarter-inch videocassette. This form was chosen for its stability, potential image quality, durability, moderate cost and small size. Four thousand videocassettes in dust-proof containers occupy about 285 cubic feet.

The Scholar Access Modules will be equipped for study of microfiche, audiocassette and videocassette. The storage area of the Collection will include humidors and cabinets for storage of the original recordings and papers. The catalogue for the Collection will be prepared along the lines advocated by the Association for Educational Communications and Technology in *Standards for Cataloging Nonprint Materials*.[1] The card recommended by AECT will be produced with the exceptions that all production credits will be added to the content description, the award category of the entry will replace the "educational level" called for by the AECT, and the date of the material will be taken as the date of original broadcast.

As to time schedule, the first task being undertaken is to publish in microfiche a listing of entries to the annual Peabody Awards competition. Listings exist for each of the years of the awards. In the early 1940s the listings consisted only of program title and producing agency. For each of the years 1942 through 1955 a mimeographed digest of entries was prepared to assist the Advisory Board in making its selections; these include a very brief (from a sentence fragment to three or four sentences) explication of program content. The digests gradually included more and more explanation, until, in 1956, the digest appeared as a bound pamphlet, as it has each year since that time. It is anticipated that the microfiche of the digests and the listings that preceded them will become available some time in 1975. Microfiche of the *entry* papers and audiocassettes of radio materials should be completed for the Scholar Access Modules by late 1975. Television material should have been re-recorded to videocassette by middle 1976.

Beginning with the 1975 competition (submission deadline, January 16, 1975), the award entries will be processed so as to be available in the Peabody Collection in accessible form at the conclusion of the awards presentation.

At this point it may be well to consider another distinguishing characteristic of the Peabody Collection. In the main, program recordings have been submitted by the producing agencies in the best recording medium available at the time. The quality of the recordings is, under these circumstances, very good. It is not surprising that some persons have suggested the Collection enter the business of providing these recordings on a non-profit basis to collections elsewhere. Others have suggested that the Collection be enriched by addition of extensive off-air recordings of contemporary programs. Both of these suggestions have been energetically resisted. While under the umbrella of the so-called "fair use" doctrine of current copyright practice, such reproduction and sale may be legal in the interests of the "advancement of science or art";[2] such practices would have adverse effects upon subsequent Peabody Awards competitions. The pervasiveness and the ephemeral nature of broadcast programs make broadcast producers very sensitive to the source and destination of all revenues which their properties occasion. To the extent that they see anyone not involved in the creative process receiving revenues from their work, they come to feel that the spirit of copyright has been violated. Feeling so, they are not likely to send more program recordings to the offending organization, regardless of the prestige associated with the awards involved.

Award Categories

As a means of describing the content of a collection too large to list in detail in an article, the program categories of the Peabody Awards along with some representative titles follow. In the first two years of the awards, award categories were fluid. The 1940 awards included "Public Service by a Network" (CBS), "Public Service by a Large Station" (WCW, Cincinnati), "Public Service by a Medium-Sized Station" (WGAR, Cleveland), "Public Service by a Small

Station" (DRFU, Columbia, Missouri) and "Best Reporting of the News" (Elmer Davis). The following year the awards categories that were to endure began to become established: Awards were presented for news, drama, music, educational programs and public service. In 1943 children's programs were represented, and "public service" for that year became "community service." In 1948 an additional category was added: "Promotion of International Understanding." In 1949 separate sets of categories for radio and television were initiated. In 1952 music and drama categories were combined into entertainment. In 1974 both radio and television entries were invited in the following categories:

1. News (reporting, interpretation and/or commentary)
2. Entertainment (musical and/or non-musical)
3. Education
4. Youth or children's programs
5. Promotion of international understanding
6. Public service (including special interest programs and projects)
7. Special (programs not included in the above categories)

The categories of the Collection can be summarized in these terms since 1944:[3]

NEWS:
more than 1300 radio entries (1944-1973); about 750 television entries.

REPRESENTATIVE TITLES [4]

"Australia Calling" MBS 1942
"Ed Murrow Talk from London" CBS 1943
"The Town Crier" KVOA Tucson, Arizona 1948
"Camel News Caravan" NBC-TV 1949

"The Vincent Cincci Execution" WIND Chicago 1962
"Kent State Coverage" WKYC-TV Cleveland, Ohio 1970
"All Things Considered" National Public Radio 1971

ENTERTAINMENT:
more than 700 radio entries; more than 600 television entries.

REPRESENTATIVE TITLES

"Standard Symphony" KPO San Francisco 1942
"FBI in Action" WGY Schenectady 1943
"Ma Perkins" CBS 1944
"Favorite Story" KFI Los Angeles 1948
"The Damon Runyan Theater" Mayfair Productions 1949
"Stop the Music" ABC-TV 1949
"The $64,000 Question" CBS-TV 1955
"The Patrice Munsel Show" ABC-TV 1957
"Liliom" KPFK-TV Los Angeles 1960
"Antigone" WNEW-TV New York 1960
"The Red Skelton Hour—A Concert in Pantomine" CBS-TV 1965
"Rowan and Martin's Laugh-In" NBC-TV 1968
"Brian's Song" ABC-TV 1971
"The Men Who Made the Movies" WNET New York 1973

EDUCATION:

nearly 800 radio entries; just over 800 television entries.

REPRESENTATIVE TITLES

"Columbia's School of the Air" CBS 1940
"Our Hidden Enemy—Venereal Disease" University of Kentucky 1942
"Invitation to Spanish" KSUN San Diego 1948
"The Nature of Things" KNX-TV Los Angeles 1954
"Hablemos Ingles" KEVT Tucson, Arizona 1955
"Marriage and Sex Attitudes" KOOK Billings, Montana 1960
"The Mystery of Stonehenge" CBS-TV 1965
"Thomas Wolfe: A Final Journey" KOAC-AM and KOAP-FM Corvallis, Oregon 1968
"D. W. Griffith: An American Genius" WAVE-TV Louisville 1970

YOUTH/CHILDREN'S:

more than 350 radio entries; nearly 500 television entries.

REPRESENTATIVE TITLES

"Music and American Youth" NBC 1941
"Junior Town Meeting" KYW Philadelphia 1943
"Let's Pretend" CBS 1944
"Superman" MBS 1946
"Listen to a Legend" WMT Cedar Rapids, Iowa 1949
"Kukla, Fran and Ollie" NBC-TV 1950

The Peabody Collection of the University of Georgia

"Big Jon and Sparkie" ABC 1951

"Children's Circle" WGBH Boston 1952

"Omnibus" (TV) Ford Foundation 1952

"Lunch with Uncle Dudley" WFIE-TV Evansville, Indiana 1959

"Misterogers' Neighborhood" NET 1968

"Zoom" WGBH-TV Boston 1973

PROMOTION OF INTERNATIONAL UNDERSTANDING:
more than 500 radio entries; over 300 television entries.

REPRESENTATIVE TITLES

"The Edge of Peace" UN Radio Division 1948

"Par le Sentier de la Melodie" KDTH Dubuque 1949

"Windows on the World" MBS 1951

"The Road to Spandau" NBC-TV 1954

"Winston Churchill: The Valiant Years" ABC-TV 1960

"Juan Bosch, Another Year, Another Talk" WCKT Miami 1965

"Transatlantic Forum" BBC 1966

"Morning in Moscow" WCCO-TV Minneapolis 1967

"Bangladesh" ABC-TV 1972

PUBLIC SERVICE:
more than 1600 radio entries; 1500 television entries.

REPRESENTATIVE TITLES

"Woven Into the Life of the Community" KNX Los Angeles 1940

"America's Town Meeting of the Air" NBC 1941

"Buy a Bomber" WDOD Chattanooga 1942

"The Brake Test Campaign" KTUC Tucson 1945

"A Square Mile of Boys" KMOX St. Louis 1947

"The Only Good Indian" KFWB Hollywood 1949

"The Navajo Hour" KGAK Gallup, New Mexico 1954

"The 60 Inch Lens" KING Seattle 1955

"American Opera Auditions" WKRC Cincinnati 1958

"Let Freedom Ring" KSL-TV Salt Lake City 1961

"The Great Gleason Express" WTMJ (TV) Miami 1964

"Firetrap" Group W 1972

SPECIAL:
nearly 450 radio entries; 200 television entries.
REPRESENTATIVE TITLES

"Metropolitan Opera" ABC-TV 1948

"Arturo Toscanini-Telecasts of the NBC Symphony" NBC-TV 1951

"Children's Letter to the UN" Voice of America 1952

"Kruschev-Nixon Debate at the Moscow Fair" RCA, Ampex (TV) 1959

"Tragedy of the Red Salmon: Jacques Cousteau" ABC-TV 1970

"Vasectomy—Is This the Unkindest Cut of All" KNX Los Angeles 1971

Notes

1. William J. Quinley et al., *Standards for Cataloging Nonprint Materials,* 3d ed. (Washington, D.C.: Association for Educational Communications and Technology, 1972).

2. Harold L. Nelson and Dwight L. Teeter, Jr., *Law of Mass Communications: Freedom and Control of Print and Broadcast Media* (Mineola, New York: The Foundation Press, 1969), pp. 222-226.

3. The assistance of Vance Trussel, a media utilization specialist in the University of Georgia Libraries, is gratefully acknowledged in preparation of these figures.

4. Selecting so few entry titles in the interests of conserving space was difficult. The authors chose titles which reflect the range of variation within entries, and which suggest program content without further explanation. No effort was made to include award winners.

Mark S. Auburn

Promptscripts of *The Rivals*: An Annotated Bibliography[1]

Listed below are some significant promptscripts and signed copies of *The Rivals*. A few are cited in the National Union Catalogue, but most are not. A check of various other catalogues to American collections has revealed no other significant promptbooks in North America. I would be indebted for information on others.

Signed copies, unless heavily annotated, are of dubious value in this sort of a listing. I have included a few unmarked copies, however, for their negative evidence (e.g., item 7: could we fairly infer that John G. Gilbert, the great Sir Anthony, was unaware of the scene between Jack and Sir Anthony in V,ii?). Promptbooks are of more value, but can only suggest the potentialities of production, never the actual practice. The more valuable ones (see, for instance, items 4, 19, 21, 26, 27, 28) were prepared specifically for a certain production or series of productions, but even they are unlikely to indicate changes which arose in rehearsal or performance after the preparation of the promptbook. Their value, like that of signed copies, is to suggest general trends in the acting tradition, not to show specific individual innovations appearing for the first time.

Citations are to *The Rivals*, edited by C.J.L. Price (Oxford: Oxford University Press, 1968), which is used in preference to Price's edition in *The Dramatic Works of Richard Brinsley Sheridan* (Oxford: Clarendon Press, 1973) only because this earlier popular edition has consecutively numbered lines within scenes and thus offers a more convenient set of references.

I follow the listing plan of Charles H. Shattuck's *The Shakespeare Promptbooks* (Urbana and London: University of Illinois Press, 1965). The list is arranged chronologically. Each entry consists of four lines. The first line gives the actor, director, prompter or stage manager with whom the book can be associated; city and theatre where used, if available; and earliest approximate date of first significant use or date inscribed in the text. The second line gives the location of the promptbook. Line three gives a physical description, usually in terms of the edition from which the promptbook was made. Line four gives a brief description of the contents.

    1. [Anonymous].　　London, Drury Lane.　　Post-1791.

    Harvard Theatre Collection.

    Marked copy of the Wilkie fifth edition.[2]

    Minimal markings except for the claim "Marked as at Drury Lane." Pencil excisions are slight, little stage business or directions. Seems to follow both Inchbald's cuts and those employed by Dibdin,[3] suggesting that the texts they print in 1808 and 1814 were already in use in the last decade of the 18th century; even then, perhaps, Julia and Faulkland had lost enough of their attraction to lose 32 lines in III.ii and 21 lines in V.i.

    2. [Anonymous].　　London, Drury Lane. "June 17, 1823."

Enthoven Collection, Victoria and Albert Museum. (Microfilm at Ohio State University Theatre Research Institute.)

Interleaved promptbook with manuscript notes; Wilkie sixth edition.

First two acts only are cut, mostly in Inchbald tradition with some cuts similar to Dolby's edition style.[4] Two interpolation of lines lost in Inchbald-Dolby cuts ("What's his damned name?"—"His damned name is Acres.") and interpolations from the first edition printed by Inchbald but not by other acting editions (in II.ii: "Yours while meretricious" and "However, when affection guides the pen...." etc.; cut in the "Third Edition Corrected"). S.d. at conclusion of III.iv calls for "Mr. Harley's song." Harley played Acres, so by 1823 at least one Acres had a singing role with other songs, besides those of II.i, interpolated.

3. Thomas Barry. New York, Park Theatre. "1828."

Boston Public Library.

Annotated David Longworth edition.[5]

Presentation copy signed "Thos Barry/Park Theatre/To Jack/1828" also bearing the signature of "Eliza Placide" on the last page. Barry, known as a tragedian, played Faulkland at the Park in the late 1820s. "Jack" may be J. H. Barnes, the low comic Sir Anthony. Pencil marks appear to be separate from cuts made in the same color ink as presentation signature. Fairly extensive cuts, particularly in the Julia-Faulkland scenes, along Dolby lines. "Asides" are cut as well as lines which might have bawdy interpretations, such as Sir Anthony's hint that Jack must have been "too lively" with Lydia (IV.ii.265ff.). Little business.

4. Goodwin and Phelps. Sadler's Wells, London. 1844.

Harvard Theatre Collection.

Interleaved promptbook from Oxberry's Edition.[6]

Extensively marked promptbook with much business indicated. Sadler's Wells was opened under the management of Samuel Phelps (1804-1878), a fine actor-manager whose work was characterized by his ability to "make Shakespeare pay"; Goodwin was his prompter. The promptbook cuts ten more lines from Julia's description of Faulkland's character (II.i.118ff.) in the already reduced Oxberry version; 14 more lines of Faulkland and Julia's painful exchange in V.i; all of Julia's lines in V.iii in favor of a silent reconciliation; and brings down the curtain at Sir Anthony's "And a good husband to Mrs. Malaprop." Additional business, probably long in use but not yet printed or recorded in an extant promptbook, appears. Sir Anthony is to bow, turn to go, return to utter another line, bow and turn again three times at the end of his interview with Mrs. Malaprop in I.ii (surely along lines Sheridan might have directed: see a similar piece of business with Sir Benjamin and Crabtree at the close of I.i of *The School for Scandal* and Sheridan's own ms. additions to the Crewe MS of the play). Lydia twits Mrs. Malaprop at V.i.251 by repeating her aunt's earlier line, "O fie—it would be very inelegant in us:—we should only participate in things," in reply to Mrs. Malaprop's decision to dash to the scene of the duel. Acres, as he will always in late nineteenth-century productions, is to show his hair in curlers at II.i.317. The challenge-writing scene includes not only the "C" or "K" business (interpolated here from Dobly), but also directs Sir Lucius to read and correct the letter. Business for Acres in the duelling scene is codified along lines increasingly familiar. He is to emphasize his fright with extra lines at V.iii.45, after having turned his backside and bent over at Sir Lucius's direction to "show him the broadside of your full front." To Jack he says "Don't be frightened," then claims he duels, but "never on a party of pleasure." In an aside he admits that he is "glad to hear" that he is "beneath" Sir Lucius's notice. He vents his spleen by driving David off the scene for being a coward at the sight of guns. And finally he is to make a topical reference, "I'll live a bachelor and pay the tax" rather than marry Mrs. Malaprop. These changes appear subsequently in almost every heavily annotated promptbook and are remarkably similar to the business printed in the 1896 Walter H. Baker edition. (See item 23 below.)

5. George Vandenhoff. New York. March, 1851.

Walter Hampden Memorial Library, Players Club, New York.

Cut Bohn's Standard Drama edition.[7]

George Vandenhoff signs this as "1850 NY" and indicates on p. 212 "Cut for Reading in 'The Evgs.'" A number of pages are wanting, but it is evident that Julia and Faulkland were excluded from handsome George Vandenhoff's "three March evenings of Sheridan at Hope Chapel" on March 24, 26, 28, 1851, as well as his repetitions in April.

6. Asa Cushman. New York, National Theatre. "October 9, 1851."

Brown University Library.

Marked, interleaved copy of Duncombe's Acting Edition [8]

Some cuts, little business. Cuts III.ii to 60 lines, cuts IV.iii following Sir Lucius's exit at line 69 (as Dolby edition), cuts V.i to Lydia's entrance, makes Sir Anthony's "And a good husband to Mrs. Malaprop" the curtain line. Cushman was a decidedly minor actor in New York who migrated to Providence and found moderate success.

7. John G. Gilbert. Philadelphia. "June 7, 1853."

Boston Public Library.

Unmarked Modern Standard Drama Copy.[9]

Gilbert's personal copy, signed, dated, otherwise unmarked. (See item 8.)

8. J.B. Wright.　　Boston, Boston Theatre.　"September 11, 1854."
New York Public Library Theatre Collection.
Interleaved promptbook using Cumberland's Acting Edition.[10]

J.B. Wright, prompter and assistant manager of the Boston Theatre, perhaps used this copy as the promptbook for the inaugural performance opening the new theatre on September 11, 1854 (as signed).[11] In this production Gilbert was Sir Anthony to his wife's Mrs. Malaprop. That Gilbert's personal copy is unmarked, and that this promptbook interpolates nearly 30 lines to Faulkland in II.i, III.ii and V.i (it does not return, however, IV.iii.69-155), is perhaps indicative of some attempts at purity which dedicated stock company actors made.

9. George Becks.　　　　Post-1857.
New York Public Library Theatre Collection.
Interleaved French's Standard Drama promptbook.

Undated, but in the hand of Becks, the remarkable collector of American promptbooks; extensive notes, cuts, additions, made at various times. Some of the interpolations of the greatest of all Malaprops, Mrs. John Drew, are noted. Two pieces of business appear for the first time—significant coughs are traded between Fag and Sir Lucius in II.ii, and a series of "halloes" grace Acres and Sir Lucius in V.iii. The letter-writing scene is expanded, and malapropisms are given to David; he announces "Captain Rabsolum" at IV.i.77 and identifies "Sir Lucifer O'Tiger" as one of the duelers at V.i.245.[12] Quite similar to item 12.

10. Harry Edwards.　　　Post-1857.
University of Michigan Library.

Marked Lacy edition.[13]

Many cuts, some business, in the copy of an American comedian of British birth who specialized in old men. Edwards (1830-1891) could have used this text in Australia from 1857 to 1865, in California from 1866 to 1878, or in New York from 1879 on at Wallack's. Returns some lines altered by Oxberry and Dibdin, but further cuts III.ii, and removes completely IV.iii.69-155 and V.i.1-128.

11. Lester Wallack. Wallack's Lyceum, New York. Post-1857.

New York Public Library Theatre Collection.

Interleaved promptbook using French's Standard Drama.

"This is the Prompt Copy used by Lester Wallack at Wallack's Theatre, 13th St. Broadway, New York," writes George Becks on the title page. Lester Wallack (also known as J.W. Lester), famous for handsome young men, portrayed Jack. Cuts appear in I.i not in any printed edition or earlier promptbook; after the coachman wishes for Jack and Lydia to be "once harnessed in matrimony" (I.i.65), Fag excuses himself and exits. Nearly half of Julia's exchange with Lydia on Faulkland's character (I.ii.118f.) is gone, along with Lydia's delightful, commonsense chiding reply to Julia for feeling indebted to Faulkland for having saved her from drowning: "Obligation!— Why a water-spaniel would have done as much." Sir Anthony's aside at I.ii.195 returns as do Mrs. Malaprop's strictures on "orthodoxy" at I.ii.257ff. (both of these lost in Dolby-FSD). The bowing returns as in item 4. The interview between Jack and Faulkland in I.ii is further cut, while another piece of business for Acres appears in writing for the first time—a cheer after "a dozen bumpers to Lydia" (II.i.355). Fag and the kitchen boy disappear at the end of II.i, while II.ii and III.i are run together as a single scene ending the second act— a change Joseph Jefferson later followed. Only 80 lines of the 135 of III.ii remain, while IV.iii.69-155 and V.i.1-128 are gone. The play ends in the manner of the Sadler's Wells version using the extra Acres business and concluding with Sir Anthony's "And a good husband to Mrs. Malaprop." But additionally, now Acre's courage is "Going!" "Going!" "GONE!" at V.iii.95.

12. George Becks.   Post-1860.
New York Public Library Theatre Collection.
Interleaved Modern Standard Drama promptbook.

Dated in Becks's hand "Burton's Theatre,/ Philadelphia/October 15, 1860." Two sets of annotations, both extensive. Darker red cuts along the lines of Joseph Jefferson's revision;[14] lighter red along earlier, standard lines. The name of T. Price (?Thomas Price, d. 1904) appears in Becks's hand. Price was associated with the Boston Theatre in the 1850s. Jefferson cuts are accurate, but probably made at a later date; there is no evidence of a three-act reduction along his lines before 1880.

13. J.H. Browne.   Boston, Boston Theatre. "May 2, 1863."
Harvard Theatre Collection.
Marked Duncombe Acting Edition.

Records for the first time several additional "oaths referential" to Acres, e.g., "Odds bottles and sips" at II.i.355. Cuts to Julia and Faulkland more extensive than heretofore, but the conversation between Jack and Faulkland (IV.iii.69-155) remains as printed in Duncombe. Ends with "And a good husband to Mrs. Malaprop." Browne was the prompter at the Boston Theatre in the 1860s.

14. [Anonymous].   Post-1865.
New York Public Library Theatre Collection.
Interleaved French's Standard Drama.

Some cuts, a good deal of business. A pre-Jefferson version with emphasis on Acres, similar to items 4, 6, 10 and 13. Part of Becks's Collection, but no other identifying marks. Becks notes that

"When Tyrone Power played Sir Lucius, at the Haymarket [,] the ladies were brought to King's Mead's Fields [sic] in Sedan Chairs."

15. [Anonymous].   Pre-1867.
Harvard Theatre Collection.
Marked Cumberland Acting Edition.

Three of four interesting cuts, no additions. Forty-five lines of the first Julia-Faulkland interview (III.ii) are gone; V.i is cut to Lydia's entrance. Thirty lines of Julia's explanation of Faulkland's character to Lydia in I.ii disappear. Of special interest are the deletions of two phrases belonging to Faulkland which may have been thought too racy and which disappear later in the Jefferson version—"amorous palming puppies" and "lascivious movements" in dancing (II.i.279, 289). The copy was a gift of merchant/publicist Henry Lee (1782-1867), so it must have been marked before 1867, perhaps in the Cambridge area (Lee's home).

16. George W. Wilson.   Boston, Boston Museum.   Post-1870.
Harvard Theatre Collection.
Interleaved French's Standard Drama.

Some cuts, much business, similar to items 4, 6, 10, 13 and 14. Wilson played Acres at the Boston Museum from 1877 to 1894; internal evidence suggests many of the changes are Jefferson-inspired.

17. John E. Owens.   Boston, Howard Athenaeum.   "November 1875."
Harvard Theatre Collection.
Interleaved French's Standard Drama.

Rather extensive annotation along three-act, Jefferson lines. Owens played Acres at the Howard Athenaeum in the late 1850s, but I suspect the book's annotations date from later than "November 1875" (as signed).

18. J. Palmer Collins.   Post-1878.
New York Public Library Theatre Collection.
Marked copy of French's British issue of Lacy's Acting Edition.
Hasty crayon excision along Jefferson lines. I have not identified Collins.

19. Sol Smith Russell.   Boston   1890s.
Harvard Theatre Collection.
Two promptbooks, cut and pasted, using French's Standard Drama.
Both promptbooks with extensive markings, annotations, business, interpolations, etc., cut along Jefferson lines and prepared by impresario Sol Smith Russell. Good examples of the Jefferson text.

20. [Anonymous].   Post-1891.
New York Public Library Theatre Collection.
Promptbook, cut and pasted in ledger, using French's Standard Drama.
Jefferson cuts, business, interpolations, arrangement and annotations. I have not identified the holograph. Good example of the Jefferson version.

21. Fred G. Ross.   "1893."
Harvard Theatre Collection.
Cut and pasted promptbook using French's Standard Drama.
This is the most easily deciphered of Jefferson versions and includes all of Mrs. Drew's interpolations as Malaprop while differentiating between her cutting (which emphasizes Mrs. Malaprop over Acres and retains Julia) and Jefferson's. Ross was the Faulkland of Mrs. Drew's company.

22. Stuart Robson.   "1895."
Library of Congress, Batchelder Collection.
Cut and pasted French's Standard Drama promptbook.

Stuart Robson's personal version of *The Rivals*, cut along Jefferson lines for the emphasis of Acres. Extensively annotated with additions, business, etc., carefully spelled out; a perfect gloss on the acting practices of this pompadour-crested mugging Acres, whose tenor voice and odd timbre made him a fortune as a lovable, eccentric country-bumpkin, capitalizing on Jefferson's popularity.

23. J.H. Barnes.   Post-1896.
Harvard Theatre Collection.
Marked Walter H. Baker edition.[15]
"'The Rivals'/As played by Jefferson with whom I played a season as Captain Absolute" reads the inscription of this not very heavily marked copy. Does make the changes necessary for Jefferson version (mostly rearranging scenes and cutting).

24. Winthrop Ames.   "1904."
Harvard Theatre Collection.
Marked and signed copy of the fourth printing of the Dent edition (1902).
Some cuts. (See items 25, 26.)

25. Winthrop Ames.   "1906."
Harvard Theatre Collection.
Marked and signed copy of Walter H. Baker edition.
Ames's personal, signed copy with pencilled changes. (See items 24, 26.)

26. Winthrop Ames.   New York, Castle Square Theatre.   December, 1906.
New York Public Library Theatre Collection.
Sides and full-typed promptscript.
Ames's scholarship apparent in this useful source. He notes the origins of many interpolations and changes, assigning some 26 substantive revisions (correctly) to Mrs. Drew or Jefferson.

Items 24 and 25 show in part how he arrived at the script for his famous 1906 production.

27. William Seymour.   New York, Empire Theatre.   June 5, 1922.
New York Public Library Theatre Collection.
Typed promptscript.

The Players Club production of *The Rivals*, an amalgam of FSD and Baker versions, cut according to the Jefferson tradition as remembered and recorded by Jefferson's friend and fellow-player, Francis Wilson. Invaluable for the Jefferson version.

28. Eva La Gallienne.   New York, Shubert Theatre.   January 14, 1942.
New York Public Library Theatre Collection.
Two typed promptscripts.

These promptscripts for the Theatre Guild production are dependent upon the "Third Edition Corrected" with cuts, business, additions, etc., separate from Jefferson, Drew or Baker. One promptscript includes music.

Notes

1. I should like to thank The Ohio State University College of the Humanities and the American Philosophical Society for grants-in-aid which enabled me to carry out part of the research for this article.

2. Sheridan corrected a copy of the first edition (London: J. Wilkie, 1775), removing some lines and revising slightly throughout to create the "Third Edition Corrected" (John Wilkie, 1776), the last text in which we can be sure he had a hand. The fourth, fifth (G. & T. Wilkie, 1791) and sixth (G. Wilkie, 1798) editions are all based on this "Third Edition Corrected." For additional information on these editions, see Price, *Dramatic Works*, pp. 58-66. The copytext of Price's 1968 edition of *The Rivals* is the "Third Edition Corrected."

3. Elizabeth Inchbald's *The British Theatre* (London: Longman, Hurst, Rees, and Orme, 1808) published the first "acting edition" of the play. With the 3,002 lines of Price's 1968 edition as a guide, Mrs. Inchbald's version is some 360 lines shorter. Her text cuts some lines from every scene but IV.ii

(the second interview of Jack and Lydia at Mrs. Malaprop's) and V.iii (the final scene); V.ii is gone entirely (as it probably was in the Covent Garden version before the second year of production: see *Dramatic Works*, pp. 49, 52); local satire disappears from I.i; novels from I.ii along with a substantial portion of Julia's description of Faulkland's character and part of Mrs. Malaprop's speech on education; Fag is reduced by 50 percent in II.i, and the coda to the scene—the hierarchical anger business with Sir Anthony, Jack, Fag and the kitchen boy—is removed; Julia and Faulkland lose 10 percent of their lines in III.ii and V.i.; Fag is cut from V.i, some of his lines going to David. Charles Dibdin's text in *The London Theatre* (London: Whittingham and Arliss, 1814) was also "taken from the promptscripts" used in the theatres-royal. Except for its restoration of the coda in II.i, it is similar to Mrs. Inchbald's text in almost all respects, but Julia and Faulkland are shortened in all by about 20 percent. Dibdin's text is approximately 400 lines shorter than the "Third Edition Corrected."

4. Thomas Dolby's edition in *Dolby's British Theatre* (London: T. Dolby, The Brittania Press, 1823) cuts 450 lines in all in a manner quite similar to Dibdin's version. Dolby also removes the second half of IV.iii, from 11. 69-155, the amusing scene in which Jack castigates Faulkland for being "a captious sceptic in love,—a slave to fretfulness and whim—who has no difficulties but of *his own* creating." Additionally, Dolby adds some new business: in III.iv, the challenge-writing scene, Acres is to mistake "addressing" for "undressing," and to ask Sir Lucius, "Does company begin with a C or a K?" Since Dolby's edition was the copytext for the Modern Standard Drama acting text (see note 9 below), it is the most influential of the early 19th-century acting texts.

5. New York: David Longworth, "At the Dramatic Repository," 1807. The first American edition; follows text based on the "Third Edition Corrected."

6. An acting text intermediary between Inchbald and Dolby, similar to Dibdin. Oxberry's *New English Drama* (London: W. Simpkin and R. Marshall, 1818) served as the copytext for two subsequent American acting texts: Boston: Wells and Lily, 1822; Philadelphia: C. Neal, 1826.

7. A collected edition; text of *The Rivals* follows text similar to the "Third Edition Corrected." Bohn's Standard Library published Sheridan's works in 1848. (I am indebted to Mr. Alfred C. Willers of the Players Club Library for calling this book to my attention, and for other courtesies.)

8. Duncombe (London: J. Duncombe, 1850) is based on Oxberry (note 6) with approximately 5 percent more lines cut from Julia and Faulkland.

9. Modern Standard Drama (New York: W. Taylor, 1846), edited by Epes Sargent, follows Dolby's edition. About 1850, this became "French's Standard Drama" using the same plates with a slightly altered main-title page, the word "Modern" omitted and the word "French's" substituted. This printing, or one from the same plates, was reoffered periodically in different dust-jackets. Mr. M. Abbott Van Nostrand, the current president of Samual French, Inc., was kind enough to confirm my supposition that the address given on the dust-jacket of French could be used to date any edition of French's Standard Drama, and to give me a list of their locations of business. These, together with advertisements and with the list of plays almost always printed on the back jacket-cover advertising other French

offerings, can be used to date any French text. I reprint the names and locations of the firm for the convenience of scholars using French texts. Samuel French, est. 1846; Samuel French & Son, 1871-91; T.H. French or T. Henry French, 1891-99; and Samuel French, Inc., 1899-present. New York offices: 292 Broadway, 1846-50; 151 Nassau Street, 1850-54; 121 Nassau Street, 1854-57; 122 Nassau Street, 1857-78; 38 East 14th Street, 1878-87; 28 West 23rd & 19 West 22nd Streets, 1887-96; 24 & 26 West 22nd Street, 1896-1910; 28 West 38th Street, 1910-24; 25 West 45th Street, 1924-present. See also my note in *Theatre Studies*, Spring 1974.

10. Cumberland's edition (London: G.H. Davidson, 1826[?]) is a line-for-line reprint of Dolby. It was reoffered ca. 1849-55 as "Davidson's Shilling Volumes of Cumberland's Plays."

11. *The Rivals* was a favorite choice for the opening performance at new theatres in America of the 19th century. Other openings include that of Wallack's National (2 Sept. 1837), Wallack's Lyceum (25 Sept. 1852), the Arch Street Theatre, Philadelphia (12 Sept. 1863), and (in Joseph Jefferson's version) the Arch Street Theatre reopening (13 Sept. 1880).

12. Sheridan himself had been quite careful after the initial failure of his play to remove malapropisms from characters other than Mrs. Malaprop. See Richard Little Purdy, *The Rivals ... Edited from the Larpent MS* (Oxford: Clarendon Press, 1935), pp. xxxii-xxxiii.

13. Lacy's (London: T. Lacy, 1857) is a distinct acting text based largely on Oxberry; it notes at IV.iii.69 that the remainder of the scene is often cut. Interestingly, Lacy's is the only acting edition to return to the "Third Edition Corrected" for Sheridan's careful italics. Samuel French & Son bought Lacy out in 1872.

14. Joseph Jefferson's three-act version of *The Rivals*, which premiered 13 September 1880 at the Arch Street Theatre, Philadelphia, with Louisa Lane Hunt Mossop Drew as Mrs. Malaprop, was perhaps the most famous version of the 19th century. His version cut Julia entirely with his first act starting with I.ii, deleting entirely I.i, and ending with Sir Anthony's exit at II.i.490. Lucy's "Miss Simplicity" speech (I.ii.323-345) was transferred from I.ii to II.ii; III.ii was cut; II.ii and III.i were run together as were III.iv and IV.i, with Acres's interpolated line, "Tell him I keep a private graveyard to bury my dead," ending Jefferson's second act. The third act consisted of IV.ii (nearly as in the original), the second half of V.i and most of V.iii, with a tag epilogue following Mrs. Malaprop's "Men are all barbarians" ending the play. All of IV.iii and the Julia-Faulkland portions of V.i were cut. Items 17-23 show this three-act version. Additional information may be found in G.H. Nettleton's edition of *The Major Dramas of R. B. Sheridan* (Boston: Ginn and Company, 1906), pp. 323-325, in W.T. Price; *The Technique of the Drama* (New York: Brentano's, 1892), pp. 183-188; in William Winter, *The Life and Art of Joseph Jefferson* (New York: Macmillan and Company, 1894), pp. 216-218; and in *The Autobiography of Joseph Jefferson*, ed. Alan S. Downer (Cambridge: Harvard University Press, 1964), pp. xxii-xxiii, 294-298.

15. The Walter H. Baker edition (Boston: Walter H. Baker & Co., 1896) was prepared from the promptscript developed by William Warren (a famous Sir Anthony and Bob Acres) and Annie H. Clarke (a famous Lydia and Mrs. Malaprop) at the Boston Museum. Baker's Plays and Samuel French,

Inc. offer this acting edition even today; no other acting edition is currently available from major suppliers of theatrical acting texts to collegiate and amateur groups. The author has seen five different productions based on this text. The text was originally printed by the "purists" among stock company actors, those who reacted to Joseph Jefferson's self-aggrandizing version. By no means pure, it essentially codified all the business developed on the 19th-century stage. I.i remains, but a good deal of local satire is gone; I.ii has several new malapropisms, but is cut along Dolby-FSD lines; II.i is reduced along similar lines, but includes more business for Acres, and the coda to the scene is expanded with a new line for the errand boy after Fag knocks him down (II.i.522): "BOY (*getting up and looking stupid*). Master kicks Fag—Fag kicks me. There's a sick cat down-stairs. I'll go and kick the cat." II.ii remains close to Sheridan, and III.i is only slightly expanded with a farcical exchange of six repetitions added to the "Not to please your father?" line (III.i.83); the last two scenes are not, as in Jefferson, run together. III.iii is cut to 65 lines, with Faulkland's delightful soliloquy reduced to five lines. III.iii is essentially Sheridan's, while III.iv has an expanded version of the challenge-writing scene and is run together with IV.i, ending with the "private graveyard" line attributable to Jefferson (see note 14). IV.ii is slightly expanded, while IV.iii consists only of Sir Lucius's challenge to Jack. V.i begins with Lydia's entrance, and retains the David-only version first printed by Inchbald (see note 3). V.ii is omitted, and V.iii has all the duel preparation business indicated in promptscripts. The play ends with Sir Anthony's "And a good husband to Mrs. Malaprop," and prints the Jefferson tag epilogue.

Richard Dyer MacCann

Reference Works for Film Study[1]

The following bibliography of reference works is intended to cover only the feature film, omitting television, educational and other special-purpose films, and technical subjects. It is as complete as possible, as of 1974, on the basis of works available in the University of Iowa library and others called to our attention. Some of the annotations are drawn in part from an earlier bibliographical article by John L. Fell in *Cinema Journal,* vol. 9, no. 1 (Fall 1969), pp. 43-48.

The list is offered as *Cinema Journal*'s own contribution to the symposium on problems of film history methodology published in this special February 1975 issue, in cooperation with the International Federation of Film Archives. We regret we were not able to include page counts or prices. Starred items are those considered by the compiler to be especially useful for a basic or beginning collection.

The bibliography is in chronological order of publication under each of the seven categories: bibliographies, dictionaries, encyclopedias, who's whos, films, film reviews, and annuals.

The rate of publication of film books has increased sharply since about 1963. Many of the works listed here did not exist ten—or even five—years ago. No doubt there are more to come, but it may be that our census has been taken very nearly at the peak of publication, and that many of the basic reference needs in film have been met.

I. Bibliographies

*Leonard, Harold. *The Film Index: A Bibliography. Vol. 1 The Film as Art.* New York: The Museum of Modern Art Film Library and the H.W. Wilson Company, 1941. Reprinted, Arno Press, 1966. Annotated bibliography covering 9,600 English language sources from 1907 to 1935: books, films, magazine articles, under subject categories.

Vincent, Carl. *Bibliografia Generale del Cinema.* Rome: Ateneo, 1953. Film publications up to 1953 organized by categories (Aesthetics and Criticism, Technique, Social and Moral Problems, etc.), with some content summary. International coverage ignoring popular magazines, with text in Italian, French and English, according to original country of publication.

Repertoire mondial des periodiques cinematographiques [World list of film periodicals and serials]. 2d ed. Brussels: Cinematheque de Belgique, 1960. Includes 786 periodicals published in 1960 in 36 languages in 57 countries or territories; postal address, initial date of publication, size, average number of pages, frequency of publication, subscription price, circulation; indexes of titles and editors.

Manz, Hans P. *International Filmbibliographie.* Zurich: Verlag Hans Rohr, 1963. Bibliography includes critical works, catalogues, reference books, film articles, film histories, and screenplays listed in English, French and German. Successive volumes for 1963-64 and 1965.

Mitry, Jean. *Bibliographie internationale du cinema et de la television.* Paris: Institut des Hautes Etudes Cinematographiques, 1966- . Projected to be an eight-part series nearly worldwide in scope, each part covering a country or group of countries. At the present time three parts have been published: France; Italy; Spain, Portugal and other Spanish and Portuguese language-speaking countries. Each part has sections on bibliography, history of the cinema, aesthetics, technique, administration and legislation, and biography.

Union Catalogue of Books and Periodicals Published Before 1914. Brussels: Royal Film Archive of Belgium for International Federation of Film Archives, 1967. Holdings of members of FIAF.

Reilly, Adam. *Current Film Periodicals in English.* New York: Donnell Public Library, 1970. Annotated.

*McCarty, Clifford. *Published Screenplays: A Checklist.* Serif series: Bibliographies and checklists, no. 18. Kent, Ohio: Kent State University Press, 1971. "All types of films are represented: features, shorts, documentaries, experimental films—even an animated cartoon. The only requirements are that the screenplay be published in English and issued commercially" (Introduction). Each entry has film title, production company and date, name of director, name of author of screenplay, source of the screenplay and location of the published screenplay.

*Rehrauer, George. *Cinema Booklist.* Metuchen, N.J.: Scarecrow Press, 1972. Fifteen hundred film books, including scripts and bibliographies, annotated alphabetically by a librarian for librarians; author and subject indexes. Supplemental volume, 1974, covers 1971-3.

Gottesman, Ronald, and Geduld, Harry M. *Guidebook to Film.* New York: Holt, Rinehart and Winston, 1972. Brief annotated lists of books, periodicals, theses, film schools, Academy Awards and other matters.

Library of University of California at Los Angeles. *Motion Pictures.* A catalog of books, periodicals, screenplays and production stills, Theater Arts Library, University of California at Los Angeles. 2 vols. Boston: G.K. Hall, 1972. Photographic reproduction of card catalogue.

Bukalski, Peter J. *Film Research.* A critical bibliography with annotations and essay. Boston: G.K. Hall, 1972. Books by category, e.g., "Film History, Theory, Criticism and Introductory Works," "National Cinemas," "Personalities, Biographies, and Filmographies," and "Bibliographies, Guides, and Indexes." Also names of film distributors and list of film periodicals, their publishers and their addresses.

International Index to Film Periodicals. New York: Bowker, 1972- . Annual bibliography, annotated and categorized, of articles in world film periodicals. Volume for 1972 indexes 61. Sponsored by International Federation of Film Archives.

Manchel, Frank. *Film Study: A Resource Guide.* Rutherford, N.J.: Fairleigh Dickinson University Press, 1973. " ... a survey designed to describe 6 popular approaches to the study of cinema, along with a practical analysis of selected books, films, materials, and information about motion picture rentals," usefully indexed.

*Aceto, Vincent, and Silva, Fred. *Film Literature Index.* Albany, N.Y. and Detroit, Michigan: Information Coordinators, Inc., April 1973, Prototype issue. American and British film periodical articles for 1971 indexed in an alphabetical arrangement. Further quarterly coverage promised.

Samples, Gordon. *The Drama Scholars' Index to Plays and Filmscripts.* A Guide to plays and filmscripts in selected anthologies, series and periodicals. Metuchen, N.J.: Scarecrow Press, 1974.

Gerlach, John C., and Gerlach, Lana. *The Critical Index.* A Bibliography of Articles on Film in English, 1946-1973, Arranged by Names and Topics. New York: Teachers College Press, 1974. A selective bibliography of 5,000 items from 60 general and 22 film periodicals under 175 topics cross-indexed by names of personalities and directors.

Batty, Linda. *Retrospective Index to Film Periodicals 1930-1971.* New York: Bowker, 1975. Includes 21 English-language magazines.

*MacCann, Richard Dyer, and Perry, Edward S. *The New Film Index.* New York: E.P. Dutton, 1975. More than 12,000 magazine articles in English about film, 1930-1970, annotated within 278 categories in chronological order; index of authors' names.

II. Dictionaries

Mitry, Jean. *Dictionnaire du cinema.* Paris: Librarie Larousse, c. 1963.

Skilbeck, Oswald. *ABC of Film and TV Working Terms.* London: Focal Press, 1960.

Thurston, C. Jordan. *Glossary of Motion Picture Terminology.* Menlo Park, Calif.: Pacific Coast Publishers, 1968.

Spottiswoode, Raymond. *Focal Encyclopedia of Film and Television Techniques.* New York: Hastings House, 1969. 1,600 entries and a survey guide to the entries.

Levitan, Eli L. *An Alphabetical Guide to Motion Picures, Television and Videotape Production.* New York: McGraw-Hill, 1970. Industry terms explained, covering such fields as equipment, filters, processing, lighting, etc.; "primarily for the advanced filmmaker."

Miller, Tony, and Miller, Patricia George. *Cut! Print!* Los Angeles: O'Hara Press, 1972.

Geduld, Harry M. *An Illustrated Glossary of Film Terms.* New York: Holt, Rinehart, and Winston, 1973.

III. Encyclopedias

D'Amico, Silvio, and Savio, Francesco. *Enciclopedia dello Spettacolo.* Rome: Casa Editrice Le Maschere, 1954-1962. Nine volumes plus index volume and supplement, 1955-65. Subjects: film, theatre, ballet, opera, circus, etc. Lavishly illustrated.

Film Lexicon degli Autori e delle Opere. Rome: Bianco e Nero, 1958-1967. A seven-volume encyclopedia of world film; "autori" include directors, writers, producers, actors, cameramen, composers, art directors, designers. The "works" section has not yet been published.

Bessy, Maurice, and Chardans, Jean-Louis. *Dictionnaire du Cinema et de la Television.* Paris: Livres de cinema, J.J. Pauvert, 1965-71. A four-volume encyclopedia of cinema subjects, actors and films.

Halliwell, Leslie. *The Filmgoer's Companion.* New York: Hill and Wang, 1966, 1967, 1970. Primarily brief credits and biographies of actors' careers, plus descriptions of many individual films and of specific themes or types of films, i.e., "family," "fantasy"—all in alphabetical order.

Boussinot, Roger. *L'Encyclopedie du Cinema.* France: Bourdas, 1967. A one-volume encyclopedia of films and movie personalities (directors, actors, script writers, choreographers, etc.).

Michael, Paul. *The American Movies Reference Book: The Sound*

Era. Englewood Cliffs, N.J.: Prentice-Hall, 1969. Biographies and filmographies for 600 players, 50 directors, 50 producers; credits for 1,000 films; award lists.

Cowie, Peter. *Sweden 1*. London: A. Zwemmer; New York: A.S. Barnes, 1969. Filmographies of directors and performers; synopses and credits of major films; index to English and Swedish titles.

Baxter, John. *The Gangster Film*. London: A. Zwemmer; New York: A.S. Barnes, 1970. Alphabetical index of actors, directors, writers, topics and real-life characters.

Svensson, Arne. *Japan*. London: A. Zwemmer; New York: A.S. Barnes, 1971. Important films with credits, plots and comments; biographies and filmographies of leading film personalities.

Weaver, John T. *Twenty Years of Silents, 1908-1928*. Metuchen, N.J.: Scarecrow Press, 1971. Silent film stars and films in which they appeared; directors and producers of silent films; silent film studios, corporations and distributors.

*Manvell, Roger, Jacobs, Lewis et al. *The International Encyclopedia of Film*. New York: Crown Publishers, 1972. General essays on history, technology, etc., together with extensive biographical entries; a large, well-illustrated single volume, arranged alphabetically.

Limbacher, James L. *Film Music: From Violins to Video*. Metuchen, N.J.: Scarecrow Press, 1974. Part 1 is expository history made up of previously published articles. Part 2 has film titles and dates; films and their composers; composers and their films; and recorded musical scores.

IV. Who's Whos

Graham, Peter. *A Dictionary of the Cinema*. New York: A.S. Barnes, 1964, 1968. A small paperback with filmographies of leading directors, some actors and others; some terms, e.g., neo-realism, free cinema, discussed briefly.

Dimmitt, Richard Bertrand. *An Actor Guide to the Talkies*. Metuchen, N.J.: Scarecrow Press, 1968. Alphabetical list of 8,000 feature-length films from January 1949 to December 1964, with cast lists; indexed by actors' names in second volume.

*Sarris, Andrew. *The American Cinema: Directors and Directions, 1929-1968.* New York: E.P. Dutton, 1968. Personal ranking of American directors, with critical essays and filmographies; a list of "best" films by year; index of films with directors and years of production; no alphabetical index of directors.

Gifford, Denis. *British Cinema: An Illustrated Guide.* London: A. Zwemmer, 1968. Who's Who of 546 stars and directors; index of titles of films mentioned; does not include films made by British directors in other countries.

Hibbin, Nina. *Eastern Europe: An Illustrated Guide.* London: A. Zwemmer; New York: A.S. Barnes, 1969. Biographies of film personalities in Albania, Bulgaria, Czechoslovakia, East Germany, Hungary, Poland, Romania, USSR, Yugoslavia; postwar film production in each country briefly summarized; index to film titles.

Bucher, Felix, with Gmur, Leonard H. *Germany.* London: A. Zwemmer; New York: A.S. Barnes, 1970. Primarily biographies and filmographies of directors, producers, performers; index of titles.

Weaver, John T. *Forty Years of Screen Credits, 1929-1969.* 2 vols. Metuchen, N.J.: Scarecrow Press, 1970. Four thousand foreign and Hollywood star film credits, 1929-1969.

*Academy of Motion Picture Arts and Sciences and the Writers Guild of America, West. *Who Wrote the Movie and What Else Did He Write?* An index of screen writers and their film works, 1936-1969. Los Angeles, 1970. Writers index; film title index; awards index.

Billings, Pat, and Eyles, Allen. *Hollywood Today.* London: A. Zwemmer, 1971. Brief biographies and credits for 370 directors, actors and others recently working in American movies; alphabetical list of films with directors and dates.

Martin, Marcel. *France.* London: A. Zwemmer; New York: A.S. Barnes, 1971. Four hundred directors, actors and others; brief comments and list of main films for each.

Schuster, Mel. *Motion Picture Performers: A Bibliography of Magazine and Periodical Articles, 1900-1969.* Metuchen, N.J.: Scarecrow Press, 1971. Includes *Photoplay*, many general and film magazines, alphabetical by actor, not annotated.

*"The Hollywood Screenwriter," *Film Comment,* Winter, 1970-71. Interviews, articles, and 50 filmographies of screenwriters. Republished as *The Hollywood Screenwriters,* Richard Corliss, editor, with additional data, Discus/Avon, 1972.

*Sadoul, Georges. *Dictionary of Film Makers.* Translated, edited, expanded and updated by Peter Morris. Berkeley: University of California Press, 1972. A select list of directors, writers and others, critically evaluated, with biographies and filmographies.

Koszarski, Richard. *The Men with the Movie Cameras: Seventy Five Filmographies.* New York: *Film Comment,* 1972. Reprints and adds 15 cameramen to the Summer 1972, issue of *Film Comment.*

Cawkwell, Tim, and Smith, John M. *The World Encyclopedia of Film.* London: Studio Vista, 1972. An extensive collection of biographies.

*Schuster, Mel. *Motion Picture Directors: A Bibliography of Magazine and Periodical Articles 1900-1972.* Metuchen, N.J.: Scarecrow Press, 1973. Articles from 340 British and American magazines and journals, both specialized and general, alphabetically indexed by name; more than 2,300 directors, filmmakers and animators; no annotations.

*Truitt, Evelyn Mack. *Who Was Who on Screen.* New York: R.R. Bowker, 1974. More than 6,000 screen personalities, primarily American, British and French, who died between the years 1920 and 1971, listed alphabetically; brief biographical sketch, including birth, death and marriage information; credits.

Hochman, Stanley. *A Library of Film Criticism: American Film Directors.* New York: Ungar, 1974. Extracts from film reviews emphasizing the role of each director; critics are those who look at film as "an art which is primarily visual"; filmographies of the 65 directors selected.

V. Films

U.S. Library of Congress. *Author Catalog, 1948-1952. Volume 24: Films.* 1953. *National Union Catalog, 1953-1957. Volume 28: Motion Pictures and Filmstrips.* 1958. The first volume attempts "to cover all educational motion pictures and filmstrips released in the United States or Canada and all current theatrical motion pictures which are copyrighted in the United States." Information given in both volumes covered releasing and production organization, length, source, summary, credits, cast during aproximately 1948 to 1957. After that the National Union Catalog covers only "those copyrighted films which have been added to the collection of the Library of Congress or for which data has been supplied by producing or distributing agencies." Instead of what appears to be in the earlier catalogues a complete listing of all Paramount and MGM features for example, there is, in Volume 53, 1958-62, only one Paramount feature, and five features and a dozen nonfiction shorts from MGM.

Scheuer, Steven H. *Movies on TV*. New York: Bantam Books, 1958- . Brief story outlines or comments, leading players and numerical ratings on films available for American television—"over 9,000" in 1976-76 edition. Formerly *TV Key Movie Guide*.

Jones, Jack Ray. *Fantasy Films and Their Fiends*. Oklahoma City, 1964. Contents: The Talkies; The 3-D's; The Serials; The Silents; Who's Who; The Silent Serials. Entries for films include producer or distributor, release year, cast and story line.

Dimmitt, Richard Bertrand. *A Title Guide to the Talkies*. Metuchen, N.J.: Scarecrow Press, 1965. Alphabetical list of 16,000 feature-length films from 1927 to 1963, giving source of each (play, novel, original, etc.) with publication data; index of author names. Two volumes.

Niver, Kemp R., and Bergsten, Bebe. *Motion Pictures from the Library of Congress Print Collection, 1894-1912*. Berkeley: University of California Press, 1967. Three thousand films made from 1894-1912, categorized by film type. Lists producers, copyright dates, lengths, contents, and sometimes casts, directors and other information. Includes both alphabetical index and subject index.

Limbacher, James. *Remakes. Series and Sequels on Film and Television*. Audio-Visual Division, Dearborn Public Library, 1969.

Thiery, Herman. *Dictionnaire filmographique de la literature mondiale* [Filmographic Dictionary of World Literature]. Gand: E. Story-scientia, 1971- . Vol. 1 of 2. Writers whose books have been made into movies; titles of the books; information about the movies; alphabetical index of titles (books and films), cross-referenced to authors. In four languages: French, English, German, Dutch.

*Munden, Kenneth W. *The American Film Institute Catalog: Feature Films 1921-1930.* New York: R.R. Bowker Co., 1971. Alphabetical list of all known American releases for this period with the following information: production company, distributor, release date, technical details (e.g., black and white, silent, 5,488 feet, etc.), credits, synopsis and source if known. The second volume is series of indexes covering credits and subjects. This is the first of a projected series to cover the entire history of American film.

*Cowie, Peter. *A Concise History of the Cinema.* London: A. Zwemmer; New York: A.S. Barnes, 1971. Volume 1, Before 1940. Volume 2, Since 1940. Although organized chronologically and partially by auteurs and genres within national cinemas, these volumes are especially useful as reference sources; many films are briefly characterized; title indexes.

Enser, A.G.S. *Filmed Books and Plays.* London: Andre Deutsch, 1971. Film title index, author index, change of original title index, 1928-1967 with supplement for 1968 and 1969.

Pickard, R.A.E. *Dictionary of 1,000 Best Films.* New York: Association Press, 1971. Films released since 1903, predominantly American, alphabetically arranged by title; story synopses, production credits.

*Sadoul, Georges. *Dictionary of Films.* Translated, edited, expanded and updated by Peter Morris. Berkeley: University of California Press, 1972. A select international list of about 1,300 films with synopses, credits and critical judgments.

Willis, Donald C. *Horror and Science Fiction Films: A Checklist.* Metuchen, N.J.: Scarecrow Press, 1972. International in scope, this book lists alphabetically 4,400 film titles and gives, for each year, length, credits and story line. Supplementary section is "Shorts (1930-1971), and Animated and Puppet Film."

Lee, Walt. *Reference Guide to Fantastic Films: Science Fiction, Fantasy and Horror.* Los Angeles: Chelsea-Lee Books, 1972. Alphabetical list with credits and costs.

Gifford, Denis. *The British Film Catalogue, 1895-1970: A Reference Guide.* New York: McGraw-Hill, 1973. "This is the first complete catalogue of every British film produced for public entertainment since the invention of cinematography" (Preface). Chronological listing in order of exhibition of film; index of titles.

Parish, James Robert, and Pitts, Michael R. *The Great Spy Pictures.* Metuchen, N.J.: Scarecrow Press, 1974. Entries are intended to be "representative." Alphabetical list gives credits and summary; introductory essay; bibliography of novels.

VI. Film Reviews

*Filmfacts. New York, semi-monthly, 1958- . Published in association with the Center for Understanding Media. Production credits, cast and players, synopsis, a critique, and excerpts from reviews appearing in several newspapers and magazines; index of titles.

*The New York Times Film Reviews 1913-1970. New York: The New York Times and Arno Press, 1970. Six volumes; film reviews reproduced chronologically as originally published; index of names and titles is volume 6; continuation volume for 1969-1970; others promised.

Samples, Gordon. *How to Locate Criticism and Reviews of Plays and Films.* San Diego: San Diego State, Malcolm A. Love Library, 1971. A small guide to film reference books and assorted criticism, including some books of reviews.

*Salem, James M. *A Guide to Critical Reviews.* Part IV (two volumes): The Screenplay, from *The Jazz Singer* to *Dr. Strangelove.* Metuchen, N.J.: Scarecrow Press, 1971. Bibliography of critical reviews of 12,000 feature-length motion pictures released 1927 through 1963; reviews cited appeared in American or Canadian periodicals and in the *New York Times.*

Wall, C. Edward. *The Multi-Media Review Index.* Ann Arbor, Mich.: Pierian Press, 1971- . Theatrical and non-theatrical film reviews listed by title and evaluated as plus or minus; 1973 volume covers more than 200 periodicals including *Variety, Classic Film Collector* and other unusual sources.

Variety Film Reviews, 1913-1970. New York: Arno Press, 1972. Nine volumes; credits and reviews reproduced as originally published; cumulative title index.

Bowles, Stephen E. *Index to Critical Film Reviews in British and American Film Periodicals. Index to Critical Reviews of Books About Film.* New York: Lenox Hill Publishing, 1975. Two volumes; length of review, name of reviewer and bibliographic data for each; key to library locations of periodicals.

VII. Annuals

Film Daily Year Book of Motion Pictures. New York: *Film Daily.* 1927-1970. Industry economic reports, U.S. and abroad; recent titles and brief credits; index of titles referring to *Film Daily* reviews; data on distributing companies, theatres, awards, Production Code, etc.

International Motion Picture Almanac. New York: Quigley Publications, 1929- . Over 300 pages of short biographies of industry figures; annual lists of films released; industry names and addresses; corporations, theatres, etc.

*Cowie, Peter. *International Film Guide.* London: Tantivy Press; New York: A.S. Barnes, 1964- . New films, production news primarily by country of origin; festivals, archives, new books, periodicals, film schools and many other sections; reports on five "directors of the year."

Film Canadiana. Ottawa, Ontario: Canadian Film Institute, 1969- . Quarterly, wih annual cumulation. Nonfiction and fiction films; indexes to Canadian productions, companies, personnel, subjects, titles.

National Catholic Office for Motion Pictures. *Films:* A comprehensive review of the year in motion pictures. New York: National Catholic Office for Motion Pictures, annual, 1965-70. Appraisals of several of the year's significant films; trend articles; the NCOMP's motion picture classification for the year.

Perry, Ted. *Performing Arts Resources.* New York: Drama Book Specialists, published with Theater Library Association, 1975- . Annual report on various research collections including film resources in Los Angeles, Wisconsin, Library of Congress, and other bibliographic matters pertaining to theatre, film, broadcasting and popular entertainments.

Notes

1. Originally published in *Cinema Journal* (February 1975) and reprinted here with permission.

David Haynes

A Descriptive Catalogue of the Filmic Items in the Gernsheim Collection[1]

Introduction

Over the past two decades film history has begun to attract serious study from academic institutions. Cinema, however rapid has been its acceptance as a legitimate field of study, is still not universally appreciated, and very little opportunity exists in most institutions for graduate-level research in the field at the present time. This situation has several basic causes.

First of all, as relatively new fields, film and its history have not yet been able to demand the significant expenditure of resources necessitated by their very nature. What progress has been made so far is the result, in almost all cases, of the work of one or two men with very little help, or even encouragement, from their superiors. With the formation of the American Film Institute, however, and the subsequent possibility of outside funds, rapid progress may come in the near future.

A second problem that faces the serious film student is the

fact that cinema is, and always has been, primarily a business. This fact causes a problem with at least two aspects. On the one hand, traditional academic administrators tend to view cinema as an industry and thus not within their field of interest or, at most, a subject for trade schools. On the other hand, since film is a business, its finest and most knowledgeable people are actively engaged in the industry and are available to the academic community for only limited periods of time. Added to this is the consideration that many aspects of the industry are guarded from public view because they involve either trade secrets or publicity myths.

A third aspect of the problem, growing in great measure out of the other two, is that there are very few museums or similiar institutions that have acquired information about film in an exhaustive way and made it readily available to the student. Again the establishment of the American Film Institute and its library will improve this situation considerably. But this is only one library located in one city, and for students working in most other areas of the country resources are not readily available. Equipment collections are rare, and carefully documented ones simply do not exist.

Despite these handicaps the serious film student can find some resources almost anywhere. Local and university libraries almost always have some film books, even if they are just industry data books and undocumented, popularly written histories and biographies. In addition to these normal resources, one occasionally finds items of significant interest to film students buried in collections and institutions that appear to have very little, if anything, to do with cinema.

At The University of Texas at Austin there are at least two examples of this phenomenon, both under the control of the Humanities Research Center. The Hoblitzelle Theater Arts Library contains many photographs of filmic interest as well as several books and a few modern copies of historically interesting films. The Gernsheim Collection of the Photography Collections contains books, periodicals, photographs and pieces of equipment relevant to the film student, as well as a few original films of historical interest.

The purpose of this paper is to describe and catalogue such books, equipment and films contained in the Gernsheim Collection as have some bearing on the cinema either as an industry or as an art.

One of the primary difficulties of dealing with the history of film is to establish some definitions and dates. Writers such as Friedrich Zglinicki[2] and Martin Quigley[3] contend that film history begins the first time prehistoric man thought that it would be nice to be able to reproduce motion. C. W. Ceram,[4] on the other hand, maintains that film history in a real sense begins with Plateau's phenakistiscope (about 1830), and that earlier experiments, while interesting, have absolutely nothing to do with cinema as we know it today.

The concept of motion pictures, as used in this paper, is dependent upon four discoveries: (1) The discovery of a method to project images in such a way that a large number of persons can see them simultaneously; (2) the discovery that the eye holds an image slightly longer than it actually appears; (3) the discovery of a way to reproduce sequential motion by many, slightly different pictorial representations; and (4) the discovery of a method to show one still picture after another rapidly enough so that the eye conceives them as in motion. All items in the Collection that demonstrate or discuss one or more of the above discoveries with the ultimate aim of the reproduction of motion are described in this catalogue.

The bulk of this paper will be composed of an annotated list of the books and equipment owned by the Collection that deal with the history and pre-history of film. The next section, however, will be a short biography of Helmut Gernsheim and an account of his collection, how and why it was formed, how he used it, how the University acquired it and how the University has used it. The significance of this section is to emphasize the fact, alluded to above, that often material of great interest to students of the film is to be found in collections and institutions that seem, at first glance, to have very little to do with cinema.

It is hoped that the information provided in this report will be useful to film students everywhere and hurry the day when some scholar will write the definitive history of one of the world's most important communications media.

The Gernsheim Collection

The Gernsheim Collection was formed from about 1945 until 1964 by Helmut and Alison Gernsheim primarily from British sources. The Gernsheims' aims were to find and preserve the important, early photographs that had survived neglect and World War II; to write about them and display them to make people everywhere aware of the possibilities for expression presented by photography; and "the foundation of a Museum of Photography, to which we would present our collection."[5]

Helmut Gernsheim was born in Munich in 1913,[6] and intending to be an art historian, he began studying this subject at Munich University in 1933. Realizing that he would have to leave Germany before he could finish his studies and wanting to have a more practical profession when he emigrated, he followed his brother's suggestion and enrolled in the Bavarian State Academy of Photography's two-year course. At the end of his training he became a freelance photographer, and one of his first commissions was to photograph the Munich Marionettes for part of a show at the International Exhibition in Paris in 1937. This gave him an opportunity to leave Germany, and after a short stay in Paris, he moved on to London where some of his pictures were displayed in his brother's gallery.

Settling in London, Gernsheim again freelanced and travelled extensively in connection with his commissions. He returned to London at the beginning of the War and was hired by the Warburg Institute of London University as staff photographer. In connection with this position, Gernsheim photographed a great number of London's most important buildings for the National Building Record. Some of these photographs were used in propaganda exhibitions mounted by the British Council and by the Ministry of Information. His architectural works were also exhibited by the Courtauld Institute of Art, the Churchill Club and the National Gallery. In 1942, he was elected a Fellow of the Royal Photographic Society of Great Britain.

In 1945, two events of great importance happened to Gernsheim. First of all, he married Alison Eames, whom he had met on first coming to London in 1938; and, secondly, he met Beaumont Newhall, the American photographic historian. Newhall suggested to the Gernsheims that important photographs should be collected and preserved. This suggestion fitted in well with Gernsheim's interest in both photography and art history. He was, of course, already convinced that photography was an art form, and he believed that if a large collection could be made and exhibited, other people would soon come to the same realization.

During the next two decades the Gernsheims collected and researched indefatigably the birth and the early life of photography. In general, Helmut collected and Alison researched. Out of this partnership was to come some 20 books, over 150 papers and several major exhibitions. A list of the books and exhibitions will be found in the appendices.

Gernsheim's collecting methods are not completely known, but the Collection contains hundreds of letters to book and antique dealers all over the world requesting information about books, photographs or pieces of equipment. In addition to the letters, there are also dozens of catalogues from booksellers and auctioneers, indicating that at least some of the items came from these sources. Some of the items have notes on them indicating where and when they were acquired. A complete copy of *The Pencil of Nature* by Fox Talbot, for instance, has a note inside the cover stating that it was bought at auction from Southbey's. Other items were undoubtedly donated.

In the early days of the Collection, Alison spent a great deal of time in the British Museum doing the research. As the Gernsheims' library grew, however, she was able to do more and more of the work at home. One of their methods of working was for Alison to find a reference to a photograph, run down the descendants of the original owner, and then for Helmut to contact each person on the list until he found the photograph.

Perhaps the most important discovery made by the Gernsheims using this method was finding the oldest extant photograph—Nicéphore Niépce's courtyard, taken in 1826.

The last reference to the picture indicated that it had been in England in the 1890s. After contacting the descendants of all the people involved, Helmut finally discovered the picture in 1952 in a trunk stored in an attic.

The first exhibition of material in the Collection was a selection of Lewis Carrol photographs shown at the Museum of Modern Art in New York in 1950. One year later a large show entitled "Masterpieces of Victorian Photography" was exhibited at the Victoria and Albert Museum in London in connection with the Festival of Britain sponsored by the Arts Council of Great Britain. This show was enlarged in terms of both size and scope and was circulated throughout Europe for the next decade. These exhibitions allowed over two and one-half million people to see, for the first time, rare original photographs by the most important photographic artists, publications by the fathers of photography and pieces of equipment by early craftsmen.

In the summer of 1963 the entire Collection was brought to the United States and an exhibition of over 1,000 items was shown in Detroit. The exhibition was so large that it was mounted in four separate buildings.

Since the Gernsheims had received very little favorable response in Europe (even in Britain) for the foundation of a museum as a permanent home for the Collection, they determined to try to find such a place in the United States. The Collection had become much too large and expensive for the Gernsheims to maintain privately; and it would cost a great deal to try to move it back to England, so it was put up for sale with the conditions that it had to go to an institution and that it could not be broken up.

The University of Texas acquired the Collection and moved it to the Austin campus in 1964. After a few months it was housed in Academic Center 5, and Dr. John Meany, Assistant to the Chancellor and Professor of Radio-Television-Film, was named curator. Dr. Meany had many other duties and, other than unpacking and becoming a little familiar with it, he allowed the Collection to stay dormant. He was, however, able to find and supply a large number of prints to *Life* for use in an issue largely devoted to the history of photography.

In 1966, Charles C. Irby was hired as Dr. Meany's part-time assistant, and the Collection was completely unpacked and put in some order. Mr. Irby spent most of his time filling the increasing number of orders from publishers and scholars. In 1967, Dr. Meany left the University and Mr. Irby was made Assistant Curator. A full-time research assistant, Anne Brown, and myself, a student at the time, were hired to fill orders and catalogue the Collection. A card file was made for the books and bound periodicals in 1968, and the cataloguing of the photographs was begun.

During the summer of 1968 an exhibition of over 500 items from the Collection was prepared jointly by the Humanities Research Center, the History Department, the English Department, the Art Department and the Architecture Department. The exhibition, entitled "Victoria's World," was shown in the University Art Museum during the fall of 1968, and an exhibition catalogue for it was published by Humanities Research Center.

In 1966 the facilities of the Collection were expanded to include Academic Center 16 as an office, and Academic Center 10 was added as a workroom in 1968. The name of the Collection was changed to Photography Collections in 1968 because several other photographic collections were added to the University's holdings.

The Photography Collections today contains:

The Gernsheim Collection—about 30,000 original photographs; 3,500 copy negatives and prints; 3,000 books and bound periodicals; several boxes of research notes; about 1,000 pieces of correspondence; and 300 pieces of photographic equipment.

The Glanz Collection—about 300 lantern slides, primarily of archeological interest.

The Goldbeck Collection—about 100,000 negatives and prints, primarily of military units.

The Hare Collection—about 3,000 negatives and lantern slides, primarily of news events.

The Jackson Collection—about 1,000 negatives and prints, primarily of archeological interest.

The Smithers Collection—about 10,000 negatives and prints, primarily of West Texas from 1890 to 1935.

Equipment and Films

As Gernsheim collected photographs, he also obtained various pieces of equipment that could be used as book illustrations and for display along with his prints. The equipment was generally amassed just because it was photographic and not in any hope to build a complete, or even significant, equipment collection. A few of these items are of specific film interest, and they are described in this chapter.

When the University acquired the Collection, the equipment was by and large stored in boxes and crates. In the summer of 1967 most of the equipment was unpacked and placed on shelves in the Collection's new office, Academic Center 16.

In order to prepare this report, all pieces of filmic equipment (both those on the shelves and those still in boxes) were found, numbered and placed together on one stack of shelves in Academic Center 16. Pieces of nitrate film found for this study were stored in a safe in the Collection's workroom, Academic Center 10.

The descriptions of the equipment and films owned by the Collection are broken up into four sections. The first section (Non-Projection) lists all items that were intended to provide the illusion of motion without the necessity of projecting translucent images upon a screen. The second section (Projection) lists and describes equipment that does project a translucent image upon a screen. The next part (Cameras) lists all the pieces of equipment that are capable of recording motion photographically. Devices that can both take and show motion are included in this section. The last section of this chapter (Films) describes all pieces of translucent photographic material that were made with the intention of showing motion.

While it is impossible to describe such diverse pieces of equipment in exactly consistent terms, an effort will be made to include all of the following information, in the following order, about each piece:

Name—of the machine or type of machine exactly as it

appears on the nameplate. If no name appears on the item, the most commonly used name will be used.

Location Number—the number assigned to the item or all items of the same type for the purpose of this report. The number will be attached to the item, if possible, or to the shelf where it is displayed. The number will indicate the location of the item. In some cases the same number will be used for more than one item, if they are all located in the same place.

Maker—exactly as it appears on the item.

Place of Manufacture—exactly as it appears on the item.

Date of Manufacture—the last patent date shown on the item. Only the year will be listed. Undated items will be given a date in parentheses ("c." means the earliest date of manufacture or published reference to the type of item).

Description—of the item. This will, of course, vary somewhat but will, in all cases, include the size (in inches, the word "inch" not written in the actual entry; the abbreviations "w." [width], "h." [height] and "d." [depth] will be used as viewed from the lensboard or the front of the instrument), the materials used, the way the item operated and the item's present condition if not perfect.

NON-PROJECTION

THAUMATROPE. This device uses the phenomenon of persistence of vision to superimpose images on both sides of a card. Typically the cards are paper discs and are manipulated by strings attached to each side. The first published description of the device was by J. A. Paris in 1827.

Thaumatrope Discs. 3/1.
 N. Carpenter, London. no date (c. 1827). Circular wooden box [(2⅞ in diameter x 1 h.) with a colored label marked "* Optical Delusion Cards * Published by N. Carpenter, London" and with a picture of a girl operating a disc] containing 10 drawn, colored paper discs (2⅛ in diameter) with strings (1¾) attached to each side as follows:

78 PERFORMING ARTS RESOURCES

SIDE 1
a group of people
several boys running
a mother
a man offering wine
several boys throwing books
a mother
a fiddler
a boy with a chick
a girl blowing bubbles
a man standing

SIDE 2
a puppet show
a dog with a can on tail
a daughter
a man on horseback
an angry teacher
a son
a dancing girl
a hen with several chicks
a dog blowing bubbles
a man sitting

PHENAKISTISCOPE. This device uses persistence of vision to create motion using a number of figures in sequential positions arranged around the outside of a circular card. The images are viewed from the back side of the card through slots next to each figure. The images must thus be viewed in a mirror. The device was invented by Joseph Plateau in about 1830 and was described in print for the first time by him in 1832.

Fantascope. 3/2.
T. T. Bury (published by Ackermann & Co., London). 1833. Cardboard folder [(10⅜ x 10) with a colored label marked "Fantascope by T. T. Bury. London, Publd by Ackermann & Co. 96. Strand." and illustrated with colored pictures from discs] containing six colored, cardboard phenakistiscope discs (9⅝ in diameter) as follows:

a man ringing a bell (14 slots and pictures)
a waltzing couple (10 slots and 11 pictures)
a man riding a bicycle (10 slots and 9 pictures)
a juggler (12 slots and pictures)
two acrobats (8 slots and pictures)
two acrobats (different) (8 slots and pictures)

Phantascopic Pantomime. 3/2.
W. Soffe, London. 1833. Cardboard folder [(10⅜ x 10) with a colored label marked "Phantascopic Pantomime, or Magic Illusions. London, Publ. by W. Soffe, 380 Strand, corner of Southampton St." with an instruction sheet, dated 1833,

pasted inside] containing three colored, cardboard phenakistiscope discs (9½ in diameter) as follows:

> Harlequin and Columbine waltzing (11 slots and 12 pictures)
> a clown acrobat (12 slots and pictures)
> Harlequin jumping through a hoop (10 slots and 9 pictures)

Phenakistiscope Discs. 3/2.

Ackermann & Co., London. no date (c. 1833). Cardboard disc (9⅝ in diameter) with 10 slots and nine pictures of a horse jumping through a hoop and 10 pictures of an acrobat flipping.

Ackermann & Co., London. no date (c. 1833). Cardboard disc (9½ in diameter) with 10 slots and nine pictures of a woman hitting a man with a bat and 10 pictures of a squirrel running in a cage.

S. W. Fores, London. 1833. Cardboard disc (9⅛ in diameter) with 10 slots and nine pictures of one frog jumping over another.

No maker, no place. no date (c. 1833). Cardboard disc (9¾ in diameter) with 12 slots and 12 pictures of a red face swallowing Harlequin.

No maker, no place. no date (c. 1833). Cardboard disc (9¾ in diameter) with eight slots and eight pictures of Harlequin and Clown dancing.

No maker, no place. no date (c. 1833). Cardboard disc (6⅞ in diameter) with eight slots and eight pictures of a boy eating a ball (apple?).

STROBOSCOPE. This device differs from the phenakistiscope in that the discs do not have their own slots but are viewed directly through a second slotted disc revolving in the opposite direction. The device was patented by Simon Ritter von Stampfer in 1833.

Stroboscope Discs. 3/2.

Alph. Giroux et Cie., Paris. no date (c. 1833). Leather covered cardboard folder [(8¾ x 9¾) with a label marked "à Paris, Chéz Alph. Giroux et Cie. Brevetes"] containing eight double-sided, colored, cardboard stroboscope discs (7⅛ in diameter), six single-sided, colored, cardboard stroboscope discs (7⅛ in diameter), and one black cardboard disc (9 in diameter) with 10 slots. The picture discs are as follows:

> a boy riding a horse and a dog jumping over a fence (11 and 9 pictures)
>
> a man playing a bass and a Cossack dancing (10 and 10 pictures)
>
> a ball and a spinning hoop (11 pictures)
>
> a log being sawed (10 pictures)
>
> a fan turning (10 pictures)
>
> a teacher hitting a student (10 pictures)
>
> a clown walking a wire (10 pictures)/pattern
>
> a man playing a bass and a Cossack dancing (10 and 10 pictures)/a snake attacking a soldier (10 pictures)
>
> a man hitting a ball with a bat (11 pictures)/black star
>
> a star in a circle (9 pictures)/a blacksmith (10 pictures)
>
> a woman standing in a tub (10 pictures)/a dancing couple (10 pictures)
>
> two men playing leapfrog (10 pictures)/a comet passing a planet (9 pictures)
>
> a man hitting a ball with a bat (11 pictures)/an ascending man passing an angel (9 pictures)
>
> a woman with a cornucopia (11 pictures)/a fan turning (10 pictures)

Stroboscope Discs. 3/2.

No maker, no place. no date (c. 1833). Cardboard disc (8¾ in diameter) with instructions for using in conjunction with a picture disc printed in English and French on a pasted-on label. The disc contains 10 slots.

No maker, no place. no date (c. 1833). Cardboard disc (8⅝ in diameter) with 10 slots.

ZOETROPE. This device consists of a slotted drum that can be rotated. Around the inside of the drum a paper band containing sequential pictures is placed (or a stroboscope disc is placed in the bottom of the drum), and when it is viewed through the slots in the drum, the illusion of motion is achieved. The device was invented by W. G. Horner in 1833 (and named "zoetrope" in 1867).

Zoetrope. 4/1.
No maker, no place. no date (c. 1833). Circular iron drum (8½ h. x 12 in diameter) standing on a wooden base (9½ h.) with an iron arbor. The drum has 13 slots.

Zoetrope. 4/2.
Carpenter and Westly, London. no date (c. 1833). Circular iron drum (7½ h. x 11¾ in diameter) standing on a wooden base (7¾ h.) with a brass arbor. The drum has 13 slots.

Stroboscope Discs (for Zoetrope). 4/2.
No maker, no place. no date (c. 1833). Paper discs (11½ in diameter) with colored pictures of sequential motion around the outside or beginning in the center and moving around to the outside.

> a canon firing (ball moves around to outside) (40 pictures)
> a lion eating a man (man moves around to outside) (27 pictures)
> a hunter shooting at some ducks (13 pictures)
> a man swimming around to outside (31 pictures)
> an acrobat turning a flip (12 pictures)
> a man jumping around to outside on a wire (32 pictures)
> a man skating around to outside (43 pictures)
> a man climbing a ladder (13 pictures)
> a fish swimming around to outside (41 pictures)
> a genie thrown out of a bottle around to outside (40 pictures)
> a cat chasing a mouse around to outside (42 pictures)
> a dog jumping for a sausage (13 pictures)

Zoetrope Bands. (Plate 3). 4/2.
Clark, no place. no date (c. 1833). Paper bands (3½ h. x 35 w.) marked "Clarke's Wheel of Life" and numbered. Each band contains 13 (unless otherwise noted) colored pictures of sequential motion as follows:

> No. 9—a windmill
> No. 12—a butterfly and flowers

No. 13—a hummingbird and flowers
No. 15—a jack-in-a-box
No. 16—a witch doctor opening and closing his mouth
No. 17—a horse jumping through a hoop
No. 19—a tight rope walker
No. 20—a steam engine
No. 21—a parrot climbing into a hoop
No. 23—a donkey eating a carrot
No. 24—a knight riding a horse (10 pictures)

No maker, no place. no date (c. 1833). Paper bands (3½ h. x 35 w.) marked with the number and title below and "Entered at Stationers' Hall." Each ban contains 13 (unless otherwise noted) colored pictures of sequential motion as follows:

1. *The Black Turn-Over.* A man flipping backwards (2 copies).
2. *The Gymnast.* A man flipping through a hoop (2 copies).
3. *The Wild Irishman.* A man dancing a jig.
4. *A Large Feeder.* A man being fed by a machine (2 copies, one incomplete).
5. *I Chews.* A large face chewing (2 copies).
6. *The Modern Man in the Moon.* A man climbing a ladder to a moonlike light bulb.
7. *The Little Umbrella Man.* A man carrying an umbrella (12 pictures) (2 copies).
8. *A Jolly Dog.* A dog with a ball.
9. *Foot Ball.* A man balancing a ball on his feet.
10. *Paddy at Donnybrook.* An Irishman with a club (12 pictures) (2 copies).
11. *Fish & Fowl.* A whale surfacing and a bird flying (12 pictures) (2 copies).
12. *Nobody's Little Game.* A frog spinning a ball (2 copies).
13. *The Cure.* A man standing on his head (2 copies).
14. *Leap Frog.* One frog leaping over another (2 copies).
15. *Steeple Chase.* A monkey riding a dog (2 copies).

16. *Such a Getting up Stairs.* An animal climbing a ladder leaning on a man (2 copies).
17. *Who's That Knockin' at the Door?* A man opens a door to a monster and then closes it.
18. *Headwork.* A man removes and replaces his head.
19. *There's Life in the Old "Donk" Yet!* A man riding a donkey (2 copies).
20. *Warm Work for Blackey.* An animal balancing on a ball (14 pictures) (2 copies).
21. *Jack in a Box.* Jack comes out of the box (2 copies).
22. *Red & Black Waltz.* A couple waltzing (12 pictures) (3 copies, one incomplete).
23. *The Coffee Grinder.* A man with a large machine.
24. *The Red Legged Ogre and His Dancing Poodle.* A dog jumping through a hoop from the head of an ogre (12 pictures).
25. *Tuck in Your Two Penny.* Two men playing leapfrog.
26. *Footsteps Beneath Him.* A small figure runs through the legs of a man.
27. *Catchee, Catchee, Catchee.* A girl throws a doll up in the air and catches it.
28. *Indian Juggler.* A man juggles four balls.
29. *More Stings Than Honey—for Bear.* A bear robbing a hive.
30. *Engine and Feline.* Two cats on top of a steam engine.
31. *You're Gettin' Very Bald, Sir.* A man having his hair cut with a machine.
32. *Sairy Defends Her Pattens.* A girl fights off a dog (11 pictures).
33. *A Well Known Domestic Tragedy.* Punch hits Judy.
34. *(title missing).* One acrobat flipping another.
36. *Don't You Wish You May Get It?* A man offering food to a crocodile.
40. *Waltz.* A couple waltzing (12 pictures).
49. *A Caution to Bad Boys.* A policeman carrying a boy away (12 pictures).
53. *A Skating Circle.* Two men ice skating in a circle.
No number. *The Ignoble Art.* Two men boxing.

No maker, no place. no date (c. 1833). Paper bands (3½ h. x 35 w.) containing 13 (unless otherwise noted) colored pictures of sequential motion as follows:

    a man on his back twirling a ball
    a steam engine turning a wheel
    a man nailing a flag to a pole
    an automatic hammer
    a man beating a drum
    a man blowing a bubble
    a caterpillar walking by a flower
    a top spinning
    a sweep chasing a cat out of a chimney
    a man chasing a ball
    a pig eating corn and growing bigger
    a man throwing a ball
    a man playing with a stick figure
    a clock telling time (clock marked "H. C. Clark 2 Garrick Street")
    a seated boy throwing a ball
    two boys on a see-saw
    a dog throwing a ball
    a man on top of a door hitting a man going through it
    a monkey climbing a ladder
    a steam engine turning a wheel
    a peacock spreading its tail
    a man on a ball juggling three balls
    a windmill turning
    one ball bouncing over another (12 pictures)
    a woman playing badminton (12 pictures)
    a man attacking a mouse with a club (12 pictures)
    one frog jumping over another (10 pictures)
    a man pulling a string and opening his mouth (12 pictures)
    a boy dancing (12 pictures)
    a man riding a horse (12 pictures)
    a woman jumping over a barrier from a horse (11 pictures)
    a railroad engine running (12 pictures)
    a frog jumping for an insect (11 pictures)

an acrobat doing a handstand and a flip (12 pictures)

a Scot rolling a hoop (12 pictures)

TACHYSCOPE. This device is like the zoetrope except that the drum is very shallow and the slots are punched in the bands rather than in the drum. This was apparently devised so that photographed motion (giving more pictures per given action than drawing) could be viewed in motion. This format also allows more pictures per band.

Tachyscope. 4/3.

No maker, no place. no date (about 1887). Circular iron drum (9½ in diameter x 1 h.) standing on a brass base (10½ h.) [with steel feet (8½ in diameter x 1½ h.)] with a steel arbor (3 h.) mounted in such a way that a string drawn across three wooden pulleys will turn the drum. A lid (same size as the drum) is provided.

Tachyscope Bands. 4/3.

Ottomar Anschütz, Lissa (Posen). no date (about 1887). Cardboard bands (2 h. x 28 w.) marked "Ottomar Anschütz Lissa (Posen)" and numbered containing gravure reproductions of photographs (and the same number of slots) as follows:

No. 1—a man running (19 pictures)
No. 2—a man riding a horse (20 pictures)
No. 3—a horse and rider jumping (23 pictures) (for use with the drum in vertical position)
No. 5—a camel walking (21 pictures)
No. 6—a soldier marching (23 pictures)
No. 7—one man jumping over another (16 pictures) (incomplete) (for use with a vertical drum)
No. 8—a man riding a horse (18 pictures)
No. 9—a goat jumping over a fence (21 pictures)
No. 10—a stork flying (16 pictures)

KINORA. In this device, patented by the Lumière brothers in 1896, individual photographic prints are mounted radially around an axle and are viewed through a magnifier as they are moved past a fiber or metal stop by a crank. Each picture is held by the stop just long enough to impress the retina and then quickly slips past the stop to be replaced by another picture. In America this type of device was very important, because Edison had all other types of motion picture devices under patent.

Kinora. 6/2.

Kinora Ltd., London. no date (c. 1896). To a wooden baseboard (12 w. x 4½ d.) is attached (by a hinge and a stop) another wooden board (9½ w. x 3¼ d.) which has the iron mechanism and the magnifying glass (with a metal hood) attached to it. The mechanism base can be elevated to about 60° by means of the hinge and fastened stop to make viewing easier. Nailed to the mechanism base is a plastic disc marked "The Kinora Registered Trade Mark Patented Throughout the World by Kinora Ltd. London." The stop is bent out of position and the mechanism is too loose to operate.

Kinora. 5/2.

The British Mutoscope & Biograph Co., Ltd., London. no date (about 1900). The mechanism and lens of this example are completely enclosed in a heavy iron casing which rests on a fluted iron base (6½ w. x 6½ d. x 3½ h.). The top of the casing opens to change reels and has a metal label marked "No. 862 The Kinora Registered Trade Mark Patented Throughout the World Caslen-Lumiere Manufactured by the British Mutoscope and Biograph Co., Ltd. London. This Instrument Not Licensed for Use With Coin Operated or Other Automatic Attachment." A separate part of the casing opens and reflects light by means of a mirror onto the picture being held by the stop. Inside the top cover and underneath the bottom of the casing is stamped "B. M. & Biograph Co. Ltd. Kinora Trademark Patent London." The lens is double faceted so that two people can watch at the same time. The crank comes out of the left side of the casing.

Kinora Reels. 5/3.

Kinora Co., London. no date (about 1900). Each reel contains 640 pictures (image size ⅞ x ¾) radially mounted between brass discs held apart by a wooden cylinder. The top disc is marked "* Kinora Co. Ltd. * London" and numbered. Six of the reels are housed in cylindrical paper boxes marked "* Kinora Ltd. * London" and two of the boxes have a pasted-in label marked "This reel of 640 pictures was taken by a Kinora Motion Camera and could have been taken by an amateur. Send to Bond's, Ltd., 138, New Bond Street, London, W., for the Golden Book of Motion Photography." The reels are as follows:

>64—men leading horses out of a burning barn
>67—a pillow fight
>123—a dancing Scot
>201—a couple doing a slapstick magic act (this reel contains two shots)
>266—a chimpanzee and his keeper
>275—an elephant and a group of men

Kinora Reel. 5/3.
B. M. & Biograph Co. Ltd., London. no date (about 1900). Exactly the same as the reels above except unboxed. No. 207 Series I—two men and a woman at a table. Incomplete.

PROJECTED

MAGIC LANTERN SLIDES. These slides were produced to be projected (typically professionally) by large lanterns. They are, unless otherwise specified, hand drawn, colored translucent images on glass bound in wooden frames. The slides owned by the Collection that were intended to give the illusion of motion fall into several catagories that will be described in the paragraphs below.

CHANGING COMICS. These are compound slides which contain one stationary piece of glass with part of the image and one or more movable pieces of glass with parts of the image or black paint applied in such a way that when they are moved the projected picture is changed or revealed more completely. The effect is generally comic in nature. Only lateral movement is possible with this type of slide.

Changing Comics. 3/3.
Carpenter & Westley, London. no date (about 1860). Three

pieces of glass (5⅞ x 2⅝) held in a wooden mount (7 x 3¾) show a lion with moving eyes and mouth.

No maker, no place. no date (this and the following two slides are listed in the London Stereoscopic and Photographic Company's catalogue [pp. 13-14] published in *The Magic Lantern: How to Buy and How to Use It* [1866]. The numbers and titles are from that catalogue.) Three pieces of glass (6¾ x 2¾) held in a wooden mount (7 x 4) show a man's face with a growing nose and moving eyes (68—Man with growing nose).

No maker, no place. no date (about 1866). Three pieces of glass (6¾ x 2¾) held in a wooden mount (7 x 4) show a dentist pulling a tooth and then the eyes of both moving (4—Dentist drawing teeth).

No maker, no place. no date (about 1866). Three pieces of glass (6¾ x 2¾) held in a wooden mount (7 x 4) show a house at night, a cat fight on the roof, and then an aroused sleeper with a broom (287—Two cats on tiles).

CHROMATROPES. These slides are composed of two pieces of circular glass with patterns painted on them that have tracked brass rings surrounding them. String belts run from the rings to a double-tracked wheel turned by a crank. When the wheel is turned the two pieces of glass turn in opposite directions thus causing an effect similar to that produced by a kaleidoscope. The whole mechanism is held together by a wooden frame.

Chromatrope. 3/4.
Carpenter & Westley, London. no date (about 1866). Two glass circles (2⅞ in diameter) with a series of ringed balls and a star pattern held in a wooden mount (9⅞ x 3¾). A paper label marked "The Chromatrope or Artificial Fireworks No. 12 Carpenter and Westley, 24, Regent Street, London" is pasted on the frame. One of the belts is missing.

Chromatrope. 3/4.
Carpenter & Westley, London. no date (about 1866). Same as above except the label is marked in part "No. 23."

RACK SLIDES. Similar to the chromatrope, in these slides one or both pieces of glass are turned relative to each other by means of a rack attached to a crank. If the rackwork is placed between the two discs, both will turn; if on one side or the other only one will turn.

Rack Slides. 3/4.

Carpenter & Westley, London. no date (about 1866). By turning the rackwork, seven concentric circles of glass (each with a planet and its moons painted on it) revolve at different rates around the central piece of glass with the sun painted on it. The total diameter of the picture area is 4⅛, and the whole mechanism is held in a wooden frame (8½ x 5⅞). A paper label marked "Mcveable Astronomical Slides. No. 1. The Solar System, showing the Revolution of all the Planets with their Satellites round the Sun. Carpenter & Westley, 24, Regent St., London." is pasted on the frame.

Carpenter & Westley, London. no date (about 1866). Two pieces of glass (3 in diameter) show a ship, the shore line, two birds, and the surface of the sea (stationary) and four birds and the foreground surface of the sea which roll and circle when the crank is turned, held in a wooden frame (7 x 3⅞). The frame is marked "Rolling Sea The Needles" and stamped "Carpenter & Westley 24 Regent St. London."

No maker, no place. no date (about 1866). Two pieces of glass (3⅛ in diameter) show a stage and trapeze (stationary) and an acrobat who turns around the trapeze when the crank is turned, held in a wooden mount (7 x 4).

No maker, no place. no date (about 1866). Two pieces of glass (2½ in diameter) with circular patterns that revolve in opposite directions when the crank is turned, held in a wooden frame (7½ x 3⅞).

No maker, no place. no date (about 1866). Two pieces of glass (2½ in diameter) with circular and angular patterns that revolve in opposite directions when the crank is turned, held in a wooden frame (7½ x 3⅞).

No maker, no place. no date (about 1866). Two pieces of glass (3⅝ in diameter) with circular and radial patterns that revolve in opposite directions when the crank is turned, held in a wooden frame (8 x 4⅞).

No maker, no place. no date (about 1866). Two pieces of glass (3 in diameter) with circular patterns that revolve in opposite directions when the crank is turned, held in a wooden frame (6⅞ x 3⅞). This example no longer works.

LEVER SLIDES. These slides have one stationary, circular piece of glass and another movable piece that is moved by a lever sticking out to the side of the mount. Circular motion through a small part of an arc (about 60°) is possible with this type of slide.

Lever Slide. 3/5.
No maker, no place. no date (about 1866). Two pieces of glass (2⅞ in diameter) show a harbor (stationary) and a ship that rolls when the lever is moved, held in a wooden mount (7 x 4½). A label marked "Ship leaving the Harbour. 1." is pasted on the mount.

WHEEL OF LIFE. This slide is a combination of a chromatrope movement and glass discs with painted or photographed images moving sequentially from the center around to the outside much as do the images on Plateau's phenakistiscope disc. Instead of a second piece of glass as in the chromatrope, however, a metal shutter with a slot cut into it was used. Thus the phenakistiscope images (now translucent) could be projected. The device was patented by Thomas Ross in 1871.

Wheel of Life. 3/5.
No maker, no place. no date (about 1871). Glass disc (3¼ in diameter) containing 37 pictures of a skater moving from the center around to the outside mounted in front of an iron disc with about 60° cut out of it, in a brass and wooden frame (10⅛ x 4¼). The mechanism is operated by a hand crank, wooden pulley and string belts. The glass disc is broken and one of the strings is too loose for the slide to operate.

Wheel of Life. 3/5.

No maker, no place. no date (about 1871). Glass disc (3⅜ in diameter) containing 39 pictures of a fish swimming from the center around to the outside mounted in front of an iron disc with about 30° cut out of it, in a brass and wooden frame (9⅜ x 4). The mechanism is operated by a hand screw, brass pulley and string belts. One string is too loose for the slide to operate.

Kinematador. 7/1.

No maker, no place. no date (about 1885). Wooden box [(14 w. x 9½ h. x 8 d.) with a pasted-on label marked "Kinematador Kinematador No. 790" with a picture of a boy operating the instrument, the maker's seal (including the initials "E. P.") and five German exhibition award seals (three of them dated 1876, 1879, and 1882)] containing a projector, two picture discs and a slide showing attachment. The projector is an iron (lens barrel, brass) magic lantern [10½ d. (to full lens extention) x 7½ h. x 4 w.] with a maltese cross intermittent movement and disc holder all mounted on a baseboard (12⅝ d. x 5⅝ w.). The movement is driven by a hand crank attached to the cross by a rod and pulley operated by a string belt. The movement drives a rubber disc shutter (about 225° of which is cut out) directly and a metal turntable (to which the picture disc is attached) intermittently (30° per shutter circle). Illumination is from a kerosene lamp. The celluloid picture discs (5¾ in diameter) contain 12 colored pictures and show: (1) two boys working on an anvil, and (2) three boys leaping over a snowman. Both are incomplete and one is mounted in the projector. By removing the disc and attaching the iron slide-showing attachment, regular lantern slides may be shown. The string is too loose to operate the movement, and the chimney is missing.

Kammatograph Discs. 6/3.

No maker, no place. no date (about 1898). Glass discs (12 in diameter) containing photographic negatives (image size ½ x ⅜) arranged in four circles near the outside of the disc. The action begins at the inside and proceeds around to the outside. These discs were used in a projector that moved the disc around one turn, then moved it laterally one frame width, then around again, and so forth. These movements were accomplished by use of the center hole (2½ in diameter) and a notch on the edge of the disc (⅛ x ⅛). They were probably designed for scientific demonstration in Kamm's Cinematographic Camera-Projector (patented in 1898). The discs show:

> two men boxing (277 pictures) (marked "No. I No 1 40.S.)
> two girls dancing (270 pictures) (marked "No. 9. 30 secs.")
> two girls dancing (259 pictures) (marked "No 10a.")
> steamboat (301 pictures) (marked "No. 19")

Biocam. 6/1.

No maker, no place. no date (about 1899). Wooden box (2 d. x 5⅕ h. x 3⅛ w.) containing a metal disc shutter (2⅛ in diameter) and a modern claw movement (for 17 mm. center-perforated film). The shutter is cut out 180°, and the aperture plate hole is ⅝ x ⅜. In front of the aperture plate is a brass pressure plate attached to a wooden cover. The device was meant to be attached between a light source and a lens. It is crank operated.

Projector. 5/1.

Pathé Frères, Paris. no date (about 1909). 28 mm. projector made of iron and steel mounted on a baseboard (20⅞ x 10⅛) marked with a threading diagram decal. The projector (20 d. x 13½ h. x 7½ w.) is hand-crank powered and the crank also turns a dynamo that supplies current to an electric lamp to illuminate the film. The reel holders will hold up to 300-foot reels. The power is transferred by spring belts. The film is transferred by one sprocket wheel with one sprocket on the outside of the wheel for every four sprockets on the inside. The double pulldown claw moves up and down constantly and is spring-loaded in such a way that the claws can return to the top of the frame from the bottom without interference, but in moving down they engage the film.

CAMERAS

Olikos. 2/1.
No maker, no place. no date (about 1897). Canvas and leather case (8¾ w. x 10 h. x 6 d.) containing an Olikos camera (7⅛ d. x 9⅜ h. x 5⅜ w.), a winding crank, an extra shutter, and seven numbered plate holders. The camera (leather-covered wood) is marked "Olikos Breveté S. G. D. G." The mechanism, powered by the crank, moves a glass, sensitized plate (2½ x 3½) across the aperture hole, up to the next level, back across the aperture hole, and so forth until 84 frames (⅜ x ¼) have been exposed. Then the exposed plate is moved to the bottom and a new plate is run through the camera. The mechanism is made of iron, aluminum, and steel; the frame counter (plate number and every eight frames) mechanism is brass; and the plate holders are aluminum. The disc shutter mounted in the machine is cut out about 60° and an extra 180° shutter is provided. The shutters are marked "737." The frame counter no longer works.

Philograph. 7/2.
No maker, no place. no date (about 1910). Leather covered wooden box (11¾ w. x 5 h. x 6¼ d.) with an ivory label marked "The Philograph Patent No. 1140-10." The mechanism consists of a disc shutter (cut out about 300°) and a drum (4 in diameter x 5 w.) that moves around and laterally through a maltese cross movement. A piece of film is wrapped around the drum, and exposures (⅜ x ¼) are made in a pattern similiar to Edison's original cylinder phonograph system. The mechanism is made of iron, steel, and brass.

Electric Gyroscope Kinematograph Camera. 2/4.
Electric Gyroscope Kinematograph Camera Co. Ltd., no place. 1911. Wooden 35 mm. camera (6½ w. x 10½ h. x 10⅞ d.) powered by a 16-volt battery. Brass plate attached to the outside of the motor door marked "Electric Gyroscope Kinematograph Camera Co. Ltd. Serial No. 120 British Patents 3798—1908 22985—1911 23505—1911 And All Principal

Foreign Countries," and an ivory plate attached to the inside of the bottom marked "Use a 16 Volt Battery for Driving This Camera." The electric drive is variable from 0-30 frames per second by a handle-controlled rheostat, and the speed is shown on a gauge at the top of the camera. Behind the speed gauge is a footage scale marked in feet to 300 feet. The disc shutter has two blades, and the angle is variable from about 95° to about 45°. The double pulldown claw is operated by a rocking cam. A viewfinder is provided. The lens and lensboard are missing. The movement could not be tested, but it appears to be in good operating order.

Aeroscope. 2/3.

Cherry Kearton Ltd., London. 1912. A wooden box (6¾ w. x 8⅝ h. x 12 d.) with a brass plate marked "The Aeroscope K. Proszynski's Patents Eng. No. 6203/10 and 9829/12 Manufactures: Cherry Kearton Ltd. 11, Haymarket, London S W," and a paper label with Proszynski's signature and the number 128 attached. The mechanism is operated by a compressed air engine supplied from a reservoir filled by a bicycle pump. One filling would run a full 450 feet of 35 mm. film through the camera. The speed was controlled by the main valve and registered on a gauge at the top of the camera (scale now missing). The disc shutter has two blades and is variable from about 175° to about 30°. The double pulldown claw is operated by a cam and lever mechanism. The film is loaded into a magazine, run through the camera, and reloaded into another magazine. The taking and viewing lenses are missing. The movement could not be tested, but it appears to be in good operating order.

Malma Familien-Kinematograph. 2/2.

Maltheser Maschinenbau, Berlin. no date (about 1910). Wooden box (3½ w. x 9⅝ h. x 8 d.) with a metal label marked "Familien-Kinematograph Malma Maltheser Maschinenbau G. m. b. H. Berlin SW. 61," and a footage scale marked in feet and meters (to 66 feet) attached. This camera-projector is operated by a hand crank that turns the take-up reel. There is no evidence that the crank ever did anything else. The shutter is a leaf which is pushed against a spring. It no longer functions. The single pulldown claw is very crudely made, unattached to the mechanism, and never could have worked very satisfactorily. The loop formers are connected and spring loaded and apparently had something to do with transferring the film, although today the way they functioned is not obvious. The lens is focused from inside the camera. An electric light bulb is provided (in a housing) for projection. In the projection mode the shutter and pulldown claw are both moved to stationary positions. All in all, no way was discovered in which this instrument could have functioned in either mode.

FILMS

The following seven filmstrips were made by E. J. Marey and Lucien Bull. They were apparently acquired by Gernsheim from Bull as each has a paper wrapper with notations initialed "L.B." The Marey films have notations on the wrappers in French which L.B. says are in Marey's handwriting. All are on non-perforated nitrate stock and are kept in a metal box marked "4 filmstrips by Prof Marey 3 ditto by L. Bull 1892-1905" in the Gernsheim Collection safe.

 Bull, Lucien, no place. 1904. Filmstrip (1⅜ x ?) (Bull's films are too fragile to be unwound.) "L. Bull 1904 Flight of a small blue Dragon-fly. (Agrion puella)."

 Bull, Lucien, no place. 1905. Filmstrip (1⅜ x ?) "L. Bull 1905 Flight of the Bee. 1500 images p/sec."

 Bull, Lucien, no place. 1905. Filmstrip (1⅜ x ?) "L. Bull. 1905 Soap-bubble bursting, struck by a 'papier-mâché' bullet from a spring gun. 800 images p/sec."

 Marey, E. J., Paris. 1892-3. Filmstrip (3⅜ x 32½) containing 22 sequential images of a mounted horse. "Cheval noir—Pas—moutè" "Date about 1892-3 L. B."

 Marey, E. J., Paris. 1892-3. Filmstrip (3¼ x 42½) containing 23 sequential images of a man swinging a pick. "Homme—Coup de pioche" "Date. 1892-3 L. B."

Marey, E. J., Paris. 1893-4. Filmstrip (3⅜ x 49½) containing 26 sequential images of a man jumping in place. "Homme saut en haut sur..." "Date 1893-4 L. B. Title is in Marey's own hand-writing L. B."

Marey, E. J., Paris. 1898. Filmstrip (3¾ x 36) containing 23 sequential images of a horse jumping over a fence. "Odette non-montée Saut." "Date 1898 L. B."

The following 13 reels of 28 mm. film were acquired by Gernsheim with the Pathé Frères Projector listed above (5/1). They could, however, have been run on any 28 mm. projector. They are composed of "covered" nitrate film and are in relatively bad shape. They are stored in two metal boxes marked "Pathe Home-Cinema Films Gernsheim Collect." in the Collection safe. Because of the deterioration they were not examined past the first few feet. All except five reels are in their original metal cans. The cans originally bore labels, but today they are either missing or unreadable. The reels will hold about 300 feet, and average about 250 feet. Only one film has a title at present and it is in English and spliced on. This film is listed first. The other information (in the descriptions below) comes from Gernsheim's notes. Apparently all the films were made by Pathé about 1910.

"The Salpae Live in the 'Colonies'"
a bullfight
a comedy about a Negress
a cartoon about a colonel
a comedy about the first air trip
a laughing pig
a woman working at a lathe
an unloading on a beach
five dancers
a nature film about dragonflies
a train trip through the mountains
firefighting on roof-tops

a comedy about a workman, a woman, and a policeman

Books

Of the 2,700 books that are a part of the Gernsheim Collection, about 275 deal exclusively or significantly with film. As Gernsheim collected he made a card file listing the books he acquired, typically including some of the publishing data as well as the author and title on his cards. He arranged the cards in sections, generally by subject. One of these sections, entitled "Pre-Cinematography and Cinematography," was of great help in preparing the present report. All of the books cited in this section were examined to see if they were appropriate to this study. In addition to this, his entire file system was checked to see if any of the other cards represented books that would be of interest here.

When the books were first housed at the University, they were shelved in no particular order. It was decided by the Collection staff to put the books in size order, give each a number, and produce an author-title filing system. This was completed by late 1968, and this file was also searched for appropriate titles.

After all the books listed in either card file had been pulled, the shelves were also searched, as were folders and boxes containing uncatalogued pamphlets, catalogues, and extracts. Thus the entire collection of published source material was gone over three times.

In addition to the books that came with the original Collection, several others from various sources have been added to the library. These books were included in the 1968 author-title card file and were pulled for examination along with the Gernsheim books.

All publications that concerned film (or pre-cinema) were gathered together and a catalogue card for each was made, with the following exceptions: (1) complete issues and volumes of periodicals, (2) exhibition catalogues, (3) booksellers' catalogues, and (4) subsequent editions of books that do not include significant changes over previous editions for which a card had been made. The following section of this chapter (A. Books by Author, Part I) reproduces these cards.

Books that contain important film information along with a substantial amount of non-film material are listed in Part II of section A.

Section B (Books Not Found) lists publications for which there is a card in Gernsheim's file, but which were not found.

The information in "Books by Author, Part I" is presented in the following order with any item that does not apply to a particular book omitted:*

Author—last name first. If a book was published anonymously and the author is unknown, the listing begins with the title. The author's name is listed exactly as it appears on the title page.

Title—exactly as it appears on the title page. All words are capitalized except articles, conjunctions, prepositions with fewer than four letters, and the infinitive "to." Subtitles are not included unless they add information.

Catalogue Number—the number assigned by the staff of the Gernsheim Collection in 1968 which indicates where the book is located.

Translator or Editor—if not shown in the "Author" position.

Binding—if other than hardbound.

Edition—if other than the first.

Publisher—exactly as it appears on the title page.

City of Publication—exactly as it appears on the title page.

Date of Publication—in Arabic numbers as it appears on the title page or in the copyright statement. If no date is mentioned in either place an estimate is made, in parentheses, based on a statement somewhere else in the book, Gernsheim's notes, or clues in the text.

---

*In the original thesis, Mr. Haynes gave very complete data on each of the film books in the Gernsheim Collection, including chapter titles, etc. For the sake of this publication, some of the information about the more well known and available books has been eliminated.

Pagination—all pages as they are numbered in the book except one fly leaf at the front and the back of hardbound books. Counted but unnumbered pages are enclosed in brackets; unnumbered and uncounted pages containing illustrations only are described below under "Illustrations"; and counted but unnumbered pages within the text (chapter titles, and so forth) are not enclosed in brackets, unless they form an entire section.

Size—of the title page in hardbound books and the cover of softbound books. All measurements are in inches to the nearest ⅛ inch. The word "inch" is not used in the actual entry.

Preliminaries—the title exactly as it appears of any non-text material whether it occurs at the front or the back of the book, in the order of its appearance. Any section not written by the author has the name of the writer after the title. If the entry requires explanatory notes, they are enclosed in parentheses. Titles that should appear and do not are supplied in brackets. Capitalization is the same as for "Title" above.

Illustrations—all non-advertising illustrations are listed. Uncounted pages with illustrations are counted, and the number of illustrations mentioned. Text illustrations are those occurring on counted pages. The number of production stills is mentioned. The subject of illustrations, if one subject dominates, is mentioned in parentheses. "Technical" means diagrams, charts and schematic drawings. "Equipment" means photos or drawings of actual machines.

Chapters—the title of all numbered chapters exactly as they appear on the contents page. If either the word "Chapter" or chapter numbers are missing they are supplied in brackets. The word "Chapter" is listed for only the first chapter. If a book is divided into parts or sections and the chapter numbers proceed from the first to the last chapter regardless of the number of parts, the part or section name and number is not included. Capitalization follows the plan described in "Title" above.

Note—on non-English books the language is noted. With English books the note is used to indicate the significance or the value of the book or to provide important information about it.

The information in "Books by Author, Part II" is presented in the following order, with any item that does not apply to a particular book omitted:

Author—last name first. If a book was published anonymously and the author is unknown, the listing begins with the title. The author's name is listed exactly as it appears on the title page.

Title—exactly as it appears on the title page. All words are capitalized except articles, conjunctions, prepositions with fewer than four letters, and the infinitive "to." Subtitles are not included unless they add information.

Catalogue Number—the number assigned by the staff of the Gernsheim Collection in 1968 which indicates where the book is located.

Volumes—if more than one.

Edition—if other than the first.

Translator or Editor—if not shown in the "Author" position.

Publisher—exactly as it appears on the title page.

City of Publication—exactly as it appears on the title page.

Date of Publication—in Arabic numbers as it appears on the title page or in the copyright statement. If no date is mentioned in either place an estimate is made, in parentheses, based on a statement somewhere else in the book, Gernsheim's notes, or clues in the text.

Of Filmic Interest—the sections or chapters in the book of specific film interest or importance, with inclusive pages in parentheses.

The information in "Books Not Found" is presented in the following order, with any item that does not apply to a particular book omitted:

Author—last name first, exactly as it appears on Gernsheim's card.

Title—exactly as it appears on Gernsheim's card. All words are capitalized except articles, conjunctions, prepositions with fewer than four letters, and the infinitive "to."

A. BOOKS BY AUTHOR

PART I

Allighan, Garry. *The Romance of the Talkies.* 186. Softbound. Claude Stacey, London. no date (about 1929). [i]-[viii], [1], 2-104. 5½ x 8½. This book has no redeeming qualities.

Allister, Ray. *Friese-Greene: Close-Up of an Inventor.* 178. Special Reissue. Marsland Publications, London. 1951. [i]-[iv], v-xiv, [1], 2-192. 5½ x 8½. This biography of one of the most important and least known pioneers is well written but, unfortunately, not very well documented.

Arnheim, Rudolf. *Film als Kunst.* 1044. Softbound. Ernst Rowohlt, Berlin. 1932. [i]-[ii], [1]-[9], 10-344, [345]-[346]. 5¼ x 8⅛. In German.

Ashley, Walter. *The Cinema and the Public.* 1029. Ivor Nicholson and Watson, London. 1934. [1]-[2], 3-43, [44]. 5½ x 8½. This short letter is an argument against giving public support to the British Film Institute on the grounds that it is controlled by the film industry rather than by the State as was originally proposed.

Baily, F. E. *Film Stars of History.* 179. Macdonald & Co., London. no date (about 1940). [1]-[10], 11-167, [168]. 5¼ x 8½. These six biographies have nothing to do with film except that the author states that he is trying to correct the inaccuracies presented by films about these characters (which he says he has never seen).

Ball, Eustace Hale. *Cinema Plays: How to Write Them, How to Sell Them.* 342. Stanley Paul & Co., London. 1917. [i]-[vi], vii-xvi, 1-141, [142]. 4 x 6½. Most of the information in this book became useless with the introduction of the talkies.

Barclay, Alex. *The Earliest Films.* 2541. Softbound. Extracted from *Discovery,* October 1958. 417-422. 8½ x 11. This article discusses the filmic activities of Friese-Greene, Marey and Bull.

Bardèche, Maurice, and Brasillach, Robert. *History of the Film.* 174. Second impression of the English edition. Edited and translated by Iris Barry. George Allen & Unwin, London. 1945. [i]-[iv], v-xi, [xii]-[xiv], [1]-[2], 3-412, [413]-[414]. 5½ x 8⅜. Written in 1935, this is one of the basic histories of the film. It expresses, of course, a rather French viewpoint.

Bennett, Colin N. *The Guide to Kinematography.* 188. E. T. Heron & Co., London. 1917. [1]-[9], 10-277, [278]-[280]. 5⅛ x 8⅛. Author's Note, Contents (Index), Illustrations (the latter two sections are printed on right-hand pages only, advertisements are on the opposite pages). 239 text photos and drawings (mainly equipment). Chapter I—Technical Survey of Ground To Be Covered   II—The Different Kinds of Kinematograph Cameras   III—Dry but Important—About Lenses   IV—Filming   V—The Dark Room, and Negative Development   VI—Printing, Tinting, Toning, Titling   VII—Photo-Play Writing   VIII—A Brief Commercial Interlude. Selling Photoplays and Films   IX—About Projectors and Operating   X—Points About Some Projectors   XI—More About Machines and Operating   XII—Electricity for Operators   XIII—The Manager-Operator   XIV—Kinematography and the Law. A general guide to the technical aspects of silent film making and exhibition, this book is aimed at the theatre owner and operator.

Bennett, Colin N. *A Guide to Kinematography (Projection Section).* 187. Sir Isaac Pitman & Sons, London. 1923. [i]-[vi], vii-viii, 1-194, [195]-[208]. 5¼ x 8¼. Foreword, Contents, Index, Advertisement. Two unnumbered pages containing one photo, and 123 text figures (mainly equipment). Chapter I—Technical Survey of Ground To Be Covered   II—About Projectors and Operating   III—The Illuminant   IV—The Condenser   V—The Rotary Cover Shutter   VI—Some Present-Day Projectors   VII—Home and Educational Machines   VIII—More About Machines and Operating   IX—Making Up the Programme   X—Electrical Notes for Operators   XI—D. C. Dynamos   XII—The Manager-Operator   (no XIII)   XIV—Kinematography and the Law. This book is a valuable source for information about silent projection in England. The last chapter is especially valuable, as very little work has been done on the legal aspects of film (other than censorship, of course).

Bennett, Colin N. *The Handbook of Kinematography.* 173. Kinematograph Weekly, London. 1911. [i]-[xi], ii-v, [vi-viii], [1], 2-271, [272], [1], 2-40. 5½ x 8¼. Publishers' Foreword, An Acknowledgment, Author's Historical Preface, Synopsis of Chapters, Blocks and Diagrams, Contents (Index). 184 text figures (mainly technical). Part 1, Chapter 1—Photographic Principle 2—Kinematograph Camera 3—Choice of a Camera Kit 4—In the Field. Scenic Work 5—Topicals 6—The Dark Room 7—Development 8—Positive Making or Printing 9—Tinting, Toning and Titling Positives 10—The After-Treatment of Negatives and Positives 11—Drying 12—Trick Kinematography 13—Rehearsed Effects Part 2, Chapter 1—The Elements of Projection 2—Persistence of Vision 3—Apparatus Used in Projection 4—The Illuminant. Electricity 5—Limelight and Minor Illuminants 6—In the Operating Box Part 3, Chapter 1—Acting Before the Kinematograph 2—Playing to Pictures 3—The Still Slide 4—The Kinematograph Camera Abroad 5—Kinematography in Colours 6—Scientific and Technical Kinematography 7—Self-Preservation in the Trade 8—Management of a Picture Theatre 9—The Law and the Kinematograph. This is one of the most complete and valuable of the resources on early film operations in the Collection.

Bessy, Maurice and Duca, Lo. *Georges Méliès: Mage.* 220. Prisma, Paris. 1945. [1]-[4], 5-205, [206]-[208]. 8 x 10⅝. In French (numbered 2793).

Bessy, Maurice and Duca, Lo. *Louis Lumière: Inventeur.* 789. Prisma, Paris. 1948. [1]-[6], 7-130, [131]-[132]. 8 x 10⅝. In French (numbered 1278).

Boll, André. *Le Cinéma et Son Histoire.* 730. Softbound. Sequana, Paris. 1941. [1]-[7], 8-125, [126]-[128]. 4¾ x 7⅜. In French.

Breton, J. -L. *La Chronophotographie.* 2534. Softbound. Reprinted from *La Revue Scientifique et Industrielle de l'Année 1897.* E. Bernard et Cie, Paris. 1898. [i]-[v], 180-216, [217]-[220]. 9⅛ x 11⅛. 46 text figures, two of which are production stills (mainly equipment). Chapitre Premier—La Photographie Animée Second—Les Nouveaux Appareils Troisième—Machines à Couper et à Perforer les Pellicules Quatrième—L'Avenir de la Chronophotographie. In French.

Brown, Bernard. *Talking Pictures.* 177. Sir Isaac Pitman & Sons, London. 1931. [i]-[vi], vii-xii, 1-305, [306]-[308], [1], 2-22, [23]-[24]. 5½ x 8⅜. Preface, Contents, Index, Advertisement. Two unnumbered pages containing one photo, and 161 text photos and drawings (mainly equipment). Chapter I—History of Talking Pictures II—General Ideas III—Film and Disc, and Silent Projection IV—Theatre Sound Systems V—Amplification, Power and Stage Equipment VI—Theatre Acoustics VII—Installation VIII—In the Operating Box—Preparing the Programme IX—Recording on Disc X—Recording on Film XI—The Studio XII—Conclusion. This early sound manual is interesting for historical study. The techniques are, of course, outdated.

Brunel, Adrian. *Film Script*. 175. Burke Publishing Company, London. 1948. [1]-[14], 15-192. 5⅜ x 8½. The appendices are the only valuable portions of this book.

Brunel, Adrian. *Filmcraft: The Art of Picture Production*. 330. George Newnes, London. no date (about 1929). [i]-[iv], v-x, 1-238. 4½ x 7. The value of this book lies in the shooting scripts and in the appendices.

Buchanan, Andrew. *The Film in Education*. 2070. Phoenix House, London. 1951. [i]-[iv], 5-256. 5⅜ x 8⅜. This book deals exclusively with the use of film and filmstrips as visual aids in traditional subject areas.

Buchanan, Andrew. *Films: The Way of the Cinema*. 155. Sir Isaac Pitman & Sons, London. 1932. [i]-[iv], v-xvi, 1-235, [236], 1-8. 5 x 7½. This book contains a little history, a little technical information, and a little criticism. The chapter on sound is interesting for historical research.

Burgess, Marjorie A. Lovell. *A Popular Account of the Development of the Amateur Cine Movement in Great Britain*. 197. Sampson Low, Marston & Co., London. no date (about 1933). [i]-[iv], v-xvi, [1]-[2], 3-212. 4¾ x 7¼. While interesting in terms of the history of amateur production, the technical aspects are, of course, outdated.

Catalogue of Kinemacolor Film Subject. 1000. The Natural Color Kinematograph Co., London. no date (about 1912). [1]-[2], 3-318, [319]-[320]. 7¼ x 9⅛. Introduction to Catalogue, The Optical Desirability of Color in Moving Pictures, Adaptability of Kinemacolor to Every Class of Subject, Kinemacolor and Its Ghostly Rivals, Explanatory Note, Index of Subjects, List of Illustrations. 64 unnumbered pages containing 64 color stills. This catalogue lists about 400 shorts available to licensees for public exhibition.

Chadwick, W. J. *The Magic Lantern Manual*. 333. Frederick

Warne, London. no date (about 1878). [1]-[8], 9-138, [139]-[150]. 4½ x 6⅞. Preface, Contents, Advertisement. 101 text figures (mainly equipment). [Chapter 1]—Introduction [2]—Optical Arrangements [3]—The Sciopticon [4]—The Pyro-Hydrogen Light [5]—The Magnesium Lantern [6]—The Lime Light [7]—Photometry [8]—Dissolving Views [9]—Dancer's Lantern [10]—The Malden Bi-Unial Lantern [11]—Chadwick's Lantern [12]—Beechey's Lantern [13]—Keevil's Lantern [14]—The Opaque Lantern [15]—Stand for the Lantern [16]—Screens [17]—Lantern Slides [18]—Production of Photographic Slides [19]—Carbon Transparencies [20]—Mounting of Transparencies [21]—Registering Carriers [22]—Statuary [23]—The Colouring of Slides [24]—Effect Slides [25]—Mechanical Slides [26]—Viewing Pictures [27]—Descriptive Lectures [28]—Reading Desk [29]—Scientific Projections. This book, published near the end of the lantern show period, contains interesting information about every aspect of the magic lantern. The sections on effect and mechanical slides are especially pertinent.

Chaplin, Charlie. *My Wonderful Visit.* 198. Hurst & Blackett, London. no date (about 1922). [1]-[8], 9-221, [222]. 4¾ x 7¼. The only value of this book is that it is an example of how a star could branch out into writing.

Charles, Edouard. *The Marvels of Animated Photography.* 2543. Softbound. Extracted from *The London Magazine,* no date (about 1905). 647-656. 6⅜ x 9⅜. This short article describes some of the operations of the Biograph Company.

Le Cinéma. 68. Softbound. Aux Editions du Cygne, Paris. no date (about 1932). [i]-[ii], [1]-[5], 6-366, [367]-[370]. 9 x 11. Ont Collaboré, à Cet Ouvrage, Préface by Henri Fescourt, Table des Matières. 32 unnumbered pages containing 24 photos, 20 of which are production stills; and 278 text figures, 103 of which are production stills. [Chapitre 1]—Précisions sur l'Histoire du Cinématographe (by G.-M. Coissac) [2]—Jules Marey et la Chronophotographie (by Dr. Noguès) [3]—Le Cinéma Parlant (by Michel Picot and Henri Charollais) [4]—Les Laboratoires de Tirage (by Georges Maurice) [5]—La Naissance d'un Film (by Louis Saurel) [6]—L'Evolution Artistique du Cinématographe (by René Jeanne) [7]—Le Cinéma en France Après la Guerre (by Jean-Louis Bouquet) [8]—Les Stars (by G.-A. Auriol) [9]—De la Photogénie Dans ses Rapports Avec les Objets, les Etres et la Nature (by Joé Hamman) [10]—Le Cinématographe et les Sciences de la Nature (by Dr. Comandon) [11]—Reportage (by J.-L.

Croze) [12]—Le Producteur, Son Rôle (by Ch. Delac) [13]—
L'Auteur de Films (by Charles Burguet) [14]—Finance et Cinéma
(by Gael Fain) [15]—Le Cinéma d'Avant-Garde (by Germaine
Dulac). In French.

Le Cinéma. 1325. Softbound. Librairie Hachette, no place. no date
(about 1925). [1]-[4], 5-64. 6¾ x 9½. Bibliographie (50 books and
articles), Table des Matiéres. 140 text figures, 29 of which are
production stills. Chapitre I—Les Appareils II—La Fabrication
des Films III—Les Applications du Cinéma IV—Le Cinéma
d'Amateurs. In French. (The name "R. Millaud" is printed at the
end of the last text page.)

The Cinema. 1013. Williams and Norgate, London. 1917. [i]-[iv], v-
xciii, [xciv], [1], 2-372, [373]-[374]. 5⅝ x 8½. One of the earliest
studies of the effects of film on public morality, this book is rather
dull and makes, as usual with this type of work, some debatable
assumptions.

The Cinema at Home. 716. Softbound. W. Butcher & Sons, London.
no date (about 1925). 1-16. 4¾ x 8⅛. This advertising booklet
contains a five-page description of the use of home movie equipment and an 11-page catalogue section describing Empire equipment designed for home use.

Clarens, Carlos. *An Illustrated History of the Horror Films.* 1006.
G. P. Putnam's Sons, New York. 1967. [i]-[x], xi-xv, [xvi], 1-256. 5¾
x 9. This is one of the best books done on a single type of film. The
production data in the Appendix is extremely useful.

Coe, Brian W. *Eighty-Two Years of Scientific Cinematography.*
2542. Softbound. Extracted from *Discovery*, August 1956. 332-338.
7¼ x 9¾. This article is a short history of scientific cinematography.

Coissac, G.-Michel. *Histoire du Cinématographe.* 460. Softbound.
Editions du "Cinéopse" and Gauthier-Villars, Paris. 1925. [i]-[vii],
vi-xv, [xvi], 1-604, [605]-[636]. 6½ x 9⅞. Préface by J.-L. Breton, Au
Lecteur, Appendices (Chronological List of French Patents from
1890 to 1900), Table Analytique (Contents), Advertisement. 136
text figures, three of which are production stills. Première Partie,
Chapitre Premier—Les Prophètes. II—Vulgarisation de la Lan-
terne de Projection III—Les Précurseurs. La Synthèse du
Mouvement IV—La Découverte de la Photographie V—La
Chronophotographie VI—Marey et Demeny VII—Edison et les
Autres Précurseurs Deuxième Partie, Chapitre Premier—Principes
Généraux du Cinématographe II—Le Cinématographe

Lumière III—Controverses et Témoignages IV—Quelques Autres Réalisateurs V—Constructeurs Modernes VI—Les Perfectionnements en Puissance Troisième Partie, Chapitre Premier—L'Industrie Cinématographique II—Quelques Notices Quatrième Partie, Chapitre Premier—Le Rôle du Cinéma Dans l'Enseignement II—La Ville de Paris et le Cinéma d'Enseignement. In French.

Coustet, Ernest. *Traité Pratique de Cinématographie*. 458. Softbound. Volume I. Charles-Mendel, Paris. no date (about 1920). 1-16, [1]-[5], 6-135 [136], 17-65, [66]-[72]. 6⅜ x 10. Advertisement, Preface, Table des Matières, Advertisement. 58 text figures (mainly equipment). Chapitre I—Notions Préliminaires II—Le Film III—Appareils Cinématographiques IV—L'Atelier-Théâtre V—Prise de Vues VI—Développement VII—Achèvement des Négatifs VIII/Tirage des Positifs IX—Montage X—Les Couleurs. In French.

Coustet, Ernest. *Traité Pratique de Cinématographie*. 458. Softbound. Volume II. Charles-Mendel, Paris. no date (about 1920). [i]-[ii], [1]-[5], 6-126, [127]-[152]. 6⅜ x 10. Table des Matières, Advertisement. 108 text figures (mainly equipment). Chapitre I—Principes Fondamentaux II—Appareils de Projection III—Lumière Electrique IV—Sources de Lumière à Combustion V—Appareils Dérouleurs VI—Salle de Projections VII—La Représentation VIII—Chronophonie. In French.

Creasey, E. *Discoveries and Inventions of the Twentieth Century*. 2530 See under: *Some Applications of Photography*.

Davy, Charles, ed. *Footnotes to the Film*. 320. Readers' Union Edition. Lovat Dickson, London. 1938. [i]-[iv], v-xii, [1]-[2], 3-334, [335]-[336]. 4¾ x 7½. This early collection contains articles by Hitchcock, Donat, Wright (I); Friese-Greene, Cavalcanti, Betjeman, Jaubert, Nash (II); Grierson, Korda, Dean, Dann (III); Bowen, Bernstein, Cooke, Hardy, and Davy (IV).

Day, Will. *The Birth of the Cinematograph: Magic-Lantern to Moving Pictures*. 2540. Softbound. Extracted from *The Illustrated London News*, August 19, 1922. 278-282. 10 x 15⅜. This article sketches the history of pre-cinema. It is, unfortunately, not very accurate.

Dench, Ernest A. *Playwriting for the Cinema*. 331. Adam and Charles Black, London. 1914. [1]-[4], 5-96. 4⅞ x 7¼. The list of production companies has value for historical research.

Description of the Cinematographe. 2673. Softbound. No publisher, no place. no date (about 1896). [1], 2-34, [35]-[36]. 6⅛ x 9½. This is a very early guide to the use of Lumiere's Cinematograph. It was probably issued as an advertisement or as a users' guide.

Dickinson, Thorold and de la Roche, Catherine. *Soviet Cinema.* 122. Falcon Press, London. 1948. [1]-[6], 7-78, [79]-[128], 129-136. 7¾ x 9½. This is the first volume of the National Cinema Series. The books of this series are valuable as national histories up to the beginning of the 1950s. They are especially valuable because of the great number of stills.

Dickson, W. K.-L. *The Biograph in Battle.* 2186. T. Fisher Unwin, London. 1901. [i]-[x], xi-xix, [1], 2-296, [297]-[300]. 5¼ x 7½. Prefatory Note, List of Illustrations, Advertisement. 92 text photos and drawings (Boer War). Considering the book Dickson could have written about his work with Edison, this is very dissapointing. It is important, however, because of the information it contains about this very early war coverage.

Donnadieu, A.-L. *La Photographie Animée.* 2669. Softbound. E. Vitte, Lyon. 1897. [1]-[5], 6-23, [24]. 6⅜ x 9⅞. Two untitled parts. In French.

Drinkwater, John. *The Life and Adventures of Carl Laemmle.* 1963. William Heinemann, London. 1931. [i]-[xii], 1-275, [276]. 5½ x 8¾. This is a popular biography of the man who became one of the most important men in Hollywood, but whose major contribution to film was his activity in breaking the film trust.

Duca, Lo. *Histoire du Cinéma.* 1189. Softbound. Revised Edition. Presses Universitaires de France, Paris. 1947. [1]-[6], 7-135, [136]. 4½ x 6⅞. In French.

Durden, J. V., Field, Mary, and Smith, F. Percy. *Cine-Biology.* 340. Softbound. Penguin Books, Harmondsworth. 1941. [1]-[6], 7-128. 4¼ x 7. This book is mostly biology, and therefore of little interest.

Eisenstein, Sergei M. *The Film Sense.* 318. Translated and edited by Jay Leyda. Second English Edition. Faber and Faber, London. 1948. [1]-[4], 5-228. 5 x 8. This is the classic book by one of the greatest Russian directors and teachers. The English edition contains much valuable information in the appendices.

Elliott, Eric. *Anatomy of Motion Picture Art.* 1737. Riant Chateau, Territet [Switzerland]. no date (about 1928). [1]-[11], 12-151, [152]-[160]. 5¼ x 7. This early critical study analyzes the art of the photoplay regardless of the final product and thus, of course, is not about film at all.

L'Encyclique de Sa Sainteté le Pape Pie XI sur le Cinéma: "Vigilanti Cura" 1936. 152. Softbound. Penser Vrai, no place. 1946. [1]-[4], 5-35, [36]. 7 x 8¼. [Chapitre] I—Ce Qui a Eté Dans le Domaine du Cinéma II—La Puissance du Cinéma III—Ce Qu'il Faut Faire. In French.

Esenwein, J. Berg, and Leeds, Arthur. *Writing the Photoplay.* 1738. Home Correspondence School; Springfield, Massachusetts. 1913. [i]-[v], vi-x, [1], 2-374, [375]-[376]. 4⅞ x 7¼. This textbook covers the silent script very completely, but the information is, of course, of very little value today.

The Film in National Life. 918. Softbound. George Allen and Unwin, London. 1932. [i]-[iv], v-xii, [1], 2-204, [205]-[206]. 7½ x 10¾. This report is important because it demonstrated the need for and recommended the creation of the National Film Institute.

Films From the British Film Institute. 1010. Softbound. British Film Institute, London. 1951. [1]-[2], 3-52. 5½ x 8½. This is a catalogue of films for rent from the British Film Institute.

Fourtier, H. *Les Tableaux de Projections Mouveméntes.* 329. Bound with three other books. Gauthier-Villars et Fils, Paris. 1893. [i]-[v], vi, 1-95. 4½ x 7. Préface, Bibliographie (six books), Table des Matières. 42 text drawings (mainly mechanical slides). Chapitre I—Les Tableaux Mouvementés II—Tableaux à Caches III—Tableaux à Tiroir IV—Panoramas Simples et Doubles V—Tableaux à Levier VI—Tableaux a Rotation VII—Tableaux Doubles et Tableaux de Combinaison VIII—Les Chromatropes IX—La Projection du Mouvement X—Théâtres Optiques XI—Projection des Tableaux Mouvementés. In French.

Fraenkel, Heinrich. *Unsterblicher Film.* 1591. Kindler, München. 1956. [1]-[6], 7-471, [472]. 6¾ x 9¾. In German.

Gastine, Louis. *La Chronophotographie.* 1453. Softbound. Gauthier-Villars et Fils and Masson et Cie, Paris. no date (about 1897). [1]-[5], 6-172, [1]-[17], 2-16. 4½ x 7½. Introduction, Index Bibliographique (18 books), Table des Matières, Advertisement. 72 text figures (mainly technical). Chapitre Premier—Chronophotographie sur Plaque Fixe II—Chronophotographie sur Pellicule Mobile III—Applications de la Chronophotographie IV—Décomposition des Mouvements par la Chronophotographie In French.

Grierson, John. *Grierson on Documentary*. 1825. Edited by Forsyth Hardy. Collins, London, 1946. [1]-[4], 5-256. 5⅜ x 8⅜. This collection of Grierson's essays and reviews is probably the best book on documentary (and film in general) in the Collection.

Guy, George S. *Tricks of the Cinematograph*. 2545. Softbound. Extracted from *The Strand Magazine*, no date (about February, 1912). 211-216. 6⅜ x 9⅜. This extract explains how two or three "tricks" (such as, a man exploding) are filmed.

Halsman, Philippe. *The Frenchman*. 1658. Softbound. English Edition. Convoy Publications, London. 1950. [1]-[96]. 6¾ x 9⅛. 24 text figures (Fernandel). This book is composed of 24 humorous questions asked in type and answered by 24 photos of Fernandel's face.

Hamburger Filmgespräche. 1350. Hamburger Gesellschaft für Filmkunde, no place (presumably Hamburg). 1962. [1]-[6], 7-64. 6½ x 9½. In German.

Hamburger Filmgespräche II. 131. Hamburger Gesellschaft für Filmkunde, no place (presumably Hamburg). 1965. [1]-[8], 9-112. 6½ x 9½. In German.

Hampton, Benjamin B. *A History of the Movies*. 1829. Noel Douglas, London. 1932. [i]-[viii], [1]-[2], 3-456. 6 x 9. This is perhaps the best history of silent studios and techniques from an industry standpoint. The coverage of the various patent "wars" is especially good.

Hardy, Forsyth, ed. *Grierson on Documentary*. 1825. See under: Grierson, John.

Hémardinquer, P. *Le Cinématographe Sonore*. 532. Léon Eyrolles, Paris. 1931. [1]-[5], 6-236. 6 x 9⅜. Préface by L. Gaumont, Avant-Propos, Table des Matières. 137 text photos and drawings (mainly technical). Chapitre Premier—Le Problème du Cinématographe Sonore: Son Histoire et Son Evolution II—Les Solutions Actuelles de la Cinématographie Sonore III—La Réalisation des Films Sonores IV—Les Appareils Industriels de Projection Sonore V—La Pratique du Cinématographe Sonore VI—L'Art de la Cinématographie Sonore: Les Applications Diverses des Films Sonores. In French.

Hendricks, Gordon. *A Collection of Edison Films.* 2544. Softbound. Extracted from *Image*, No. 3, September 1959. 156-164. 7 x 10. Editorial Note. 17 text photos, 16 of which are production stills. This condensation of a study by Hendricks lists and describes 16 short films made by Edison between 1894 and 1897 and now owned by George Eastman House.

Hepworth, Cecil M. *Animated Photography: The A B C of the Cinematograph.* 660. Hazell, Watson, & Viney, London. 1897. [i]-[ii], iii-vi, 1-108, vii-xx, [xxi]-[xxii]. 4⅝ x 7⅛. Contents, Classified Index to Advertisements. 23 text drawings (equipment). Chapter I—Cinematograph Pictures   II—The Optical System   III—The Mechanical System   IV—Intermittent Mechanism   V—Continuous Mechanism   VI—The Shutter   VII—Illuminants: The Limelight   VIII—The Electric Arc Light   IX—Combination of Lantern and Cinematograph   X—Precautions Against Danger   XI—Hints and Cautions: Care of Cinefilms, etc.   XII—Cinematographic Cameras   XIII—On Taking Animated Photographs   XIV—Developing, Printing, etc.   XV—Conclusion. This very early popular guide to cinematography is doubly interesting because of the equipment advertisements therein.

Hepworth, Cecil M. *Came the Dawn.* 1660. Phoenix House, London. 1951. [1]-[4], 5-207, [208]. 5⅜ x 8½. This is a popularly written autobiography of one of Britain's pioneer filmmakers.

Hopwood, Henry V. *Living Pictures.* 620. Optician & Photographic Trades Review, London. 1899. i-xii, [1], 2-275, [276], xiii-xxvii. 5⅜ x 8. Contents, Preface, Appendix I (Chronological Digest of British Patents), Appendix II (Annotated Bibliography: 145 books and articles), General Index. 242 text figures (mainly equipment). Chapter I—Persistence of Vision and Continued Perception of the Same Object   II—Illusion of Motion, Produced by Successive Views of Slightly Varying Diagrams   III—Chronophotography and the Practical Development of the Living Picture   IV—Present Day Cameras and Projection Apparatus   V—Films: Their Production and Treatment   VI—Exhibiting Hints, Accessories, Lighting, Accidents, etc.   VII—Past, Present, and Future. This is one of the most valuable technical sources in the Collection. It gives very detailed descriptions of all of the forerunners of film and most of the contemporary machines.

Hutton, C. Clayton. *The Making of Henry V.* 1647. No publisher, London. no date (about 1944). [1]-[7], 8-72. 5⅞ x 9. This little book is of no particular interest to the scholar.

Jarratt, Vernon. *The Italian Cinema.* 118. Falcon Press, London. 1951. [i]-[iv], v, [vi], vii-ix, [x], 11-115, [116]. 7⅜ x 9¾. This volume of the National Cinema Series is strong enough in the pre-war years to be significant. The author cannot, of course, discuss neo-realism in historical perspective.

Jones, Bernard E. *The Cinematograph Book.* 2193. Cassell and Company, London. 1915. [i]-[v], vi-ix, [1], 2-216. 4¾ x 7½. The information in this book is only of historical interest.

Kalbus, Oskar. *Vom Werden Deutscher Filmkunst.* 1312. 2. Teil: *Der Tonfilm.* Cigaretten=Bilderdienst, Altona=Bahrenfeld. 1935. [1]-[2], 3-136. 8¾ x 12¼. In German.

Kempe, Fritz. *Soziale Ambition des Fernsehens und der Film.* 2532. Softbound. Reprinted from *Film·Bild·Ton,* Heft 9. 1957. No publisher, no place. no date (about 1957). [1]-[8]. 6⅝ x 9¼. Seven production stills (from *Junggesellen-Party*). In German.

Kinematograph Year Book: 1924. 2302. Kinematograph Publications, London. 1924. [i]-[vi], [1], 2-528, [529]-[534]. 5⅛ x 8. This very valuable research tool lists, among other things, all the films released during the year and all the theatres operating in Britain and Ireland.

The Kinematograph Year Book Diary and Directory: 1916. 1140. The Kinematograph & Lantern Weekly, London. no date (about 1917). 5-468. 5 x 8. This edition of the *Year Book* contains no chapters as such. A great deal of information of a technical and business nature is given in tables and articles throughout the book. The most valuable sections for the modern scholar are the directory sections that list manufacturers, renters, theatres and so forth. Also of lasting value is a section of 13 articles describing films made by top producers (authors include Griffith and Porter).

Klein, Adrian Bernard. *Colour Cinematography.* 1820. Chapman & Hall, London. 1936. [i]-[iv], v-xii, [1]-[2], 3-350. 5¼ x 8½. Preface, Contents, Historical Summary, Appendix I (Lenses Used in Technicolor by H. W. Lee), Appendix II (Glossary), Appendix III (Klein Tri-colour Camera), Appendix IV (Harmonicolor Process), Personal Name Index, Subject Index. 46 unnumbered pages containing 55 figures (equipment). Chapter I—The Theoretical Basis II—Additive Processes   III—Subtractive Processes   IV—Colour-Cameras and Beam-Splitting Systems   V—Bipack   VI—Analysis and Synthesis Problems   VII—The Phenomena of Colour Vision and the Making of Films in Colour. This is an exhaustive study of the technical aspects of color film up to the mid-thirties written by one of the important investigators.

Knight, Arthur. *The Liveliest Art.* 848. Macmillan Company, New York. 1957. [i]-[vi], vii-xiv, 1-383, [384]-[385]. 5½ x 8¼. This is probably the most widely used text for film courses and is badly in need of revision.

Kracauer, Siegfried. *From Caligari to Hitler.* 2527. Second Printing. Princeton University Press, Princeton. 1947. [i]-[iv], v-xii, [1]-[2], 3-361, [362]-[364]. 5¾ x 9⅛. Kracauer's classic study of the films produced by Germany correlated with the psychological temper of the people is still the best study of its kind.

Kubnick, Henri. *Les Frères Lumière.* 2244. Softbound. Librairie Plon, Paris. no date (about 1938). [1]-[7], 8-91, [92]-[96]. 5½ x 8. In French.

Langlands, Thomas F. *Popular Cinematography.* 1901. W. & G. Foyle, London. 1926. [i]-[viii], v-x, 1-95, [96]. 4¾ x 7⅛. This is one of the earliest manuals for amateur cinematography.

Leyda, Jay. *Kino.* 2152. George Allen & Unwin, London. 1960. [1]-[11], 12-493, [494], 1-34. 5¾ x 9⅛. This beautifully documented book is an ideal national history. The production data is especially valuable to the historian.

Liesegang, F. Paul. *Handbuch der Praktischen Kinematographie.* 2215. Sechste, umgearbeitete Auflage. M. Eger, Leipzig. 1919. [i]-[vi], vii-viii, 1-353, [354]-[356]. 5½ x 8¾. In German.

Liesegang, F. Paul. *Zahlen und Quellen.* 1506. Deutsches Druck- und Verlagshaus, Berlin. 1926. [1]-[4], 5-125, [126]-[129]. 4⅝ x 6⅜. In German.

Lindgren, Ernest. *The Art of the Film.* 849. Readers Union Edition. George Allen & Unwin, London. 1950. [i]-[iv], v-xiv, [1]-[2], 3-242. 5⅜ x 8½. While a good overview of the technical aspects of film production, this book is somewhat outdated.

Lloyd, Blodwen, ed. *Science in Films I.* 1874. Sampson Low, Marston & Co., London. 1948. [i]-[iv], v-xvi, [1]-[2], 3-238, [239]-[240]. 5⅜ x 8½. The value of this book is the Reference Section which lists the scientific films, production companies, libraries, and so forth by country.

Löbel, Léopold. *La Technique Cinématographique.* 2222. H. Dunod et E. Pinat, Paris. 1912. 1-8, [i]-[v], vi-xii, 1-324. 6 x 9½. Advertisement, Préface, Introduction, Table Analytique des Matières, Table Alphabétique des Matières. Première Partie, Chapitre I—Le Film II—Le Poste de Projection III—Le Mécanisme de Projection IV—Les Sources de Lumière V—L'Objectif VI—Installation des Appareils VII—La Représentation Cinématographique Deuxième Partie, Chapitre I—L'Atelier Théâtre de Prise de Vue II—Les Appareils de Prise de Vue et Leurs Accessoires III—L'Opération de Prise de Vue IV—Les Films Négatifs. Leur Contrôle et Leur Développement V—L'Arrangement des Négatifs VI—La Perforation VII—Le Tirage des Positifs VIII—Les Titres IX—Le Développement des Positifs X—Les Virages et les Teintures XI—Le Coloris XII—Le Montage XIII—Installation Générale de l'Usine. In French.

Low, Rachael. *The History of the British Film: 1906-1914.* 128. George Allen & Unwin, London. 1949. [1]-[4], 5-309, [310]-[312]. 6 x 9¼. This book is the second volume of Low's classic history, covering the British film from 1896 to 1918.

Low, Rachael. *The History of the British Film: 1914-1918.* 129. George Allen & Unwin, London. 1950. [1]-[4], 5-332, [333]-[336]. 6 x 9¼. This book is the third volume of Low's classic history, covering the British film from 1896 to 1918.

Low, Rachael, and Manvell, Roger. *The History of the British Film: 1896-1906.* 134. George Allen & Unwin, London. 1948. [i]-[iv], 7-136. 6 x 9¼. This is the first volume of Low's classic history of the British film from 1896-1918. The series is an outstanding monument to careful and well-documented research.

The Magic Lantern; Its History and Effects. 1094. A. and S. Joseph, Myers, and Co., London. 1854. [1]-[5], 6-50. 4¼ x 7. 10 text drawings (mainly equipment). [Chapter 1]—The Magic Lantern [2]—Description of a New Self-Adjusting Apparatus. This small book is interesting because it describes some of the effects that could be presented by projection in the middle of the 19th century.

Magnan, A. *Cinématographie Jusqu'à 12000 Vues par Seconde.* 2536. Softbound. Hermann & Cie, Paris. 1932. [i]-[ii], [1]-[3], 4-19, [20]-[22]. 6½ x 9⅞. 28 unnumbered pages containing 20 photos, 17 of which are production stills; and seven text drawings. In French.

Magnan, M. A. *Premiers Essais de Cinématographie Ultra-Rapide.* 2535. Softbound. Hermann et Cie, Paris. 1932. [i]-[ii], [1]-[3], 4-26, [27]-[28]. 6½ x 9⅞. In French.

Manvell, Roger. *Film.* 338. Softbound. Penguin Books, no place (probably Harmondsworth). 1944. [1]-[4], 5-192. 4¼ x 7. While this book is outdated, the general critical principles are relatively valid.

Manvell, Roger. *Film.* 339. Softbound. Revised Edition. Penguin Books, Harmondsworth. 1946. [1]-[4], 5-240. 4⅜ x 7. As in the first edition, the general critical principles are valid, but the particular criticisms seem very dated.

Manvell, Roger. *A Seat at the Cinema.* 838. Evans Brothers, London. 1951. [1]-[12], 13-192. 5½ x 8½. This introductory book is interesting in that Manvell discusses the cinema (industry) and film (communication) as separate things.

Marey, J. *La Chronophotographie.* 1441. Softbound. Gauthier-Villars, Paris. 1899. [i]-[ii], [1]-[5], 6-40. 5⅝ x 9. 23 text figures, six of which are Marey's plates. Six untitled sections. In French.

Marey, E. J. *Comparative Locomotion of Different Animals.* 1418. Translated from *La Nature,* September 2, 1893; vol. XXI, pp. 215-218. Softbound. Extracted from *Annual Report of the Smithsonian Institution: 1893.* Washington. 1894. 501-504. 5¾ x 8⅞. Six unnumbered pages containing 10 photos. This paper is valuable because it discusses one of the earliest uses of photography to demonstrate motion for scientific purposes. The work of Marey, Bull and Muybridge is very important for this reason.

Marey, E.-J. *Le Mouvement.* 2240. G. Masson, Paris. 1894. [i]-[v], vi, 1-335, [336]. 4⅞ x 7¾. Avant-Propos, Table des Matières, Table des Gravures, Table Analytique. Six unnumbered pages containing 44 photos (sequential motion), and 214 text figures. Chapitre Premier—Du Temps   II—De l'Espace   III—Le Mouvement   IV—Chronophotographie sur Plaque Fixe   V—Description et Emploi du Chronophotographe sur Plaque Fixe   VI—Applications de la Chronophotographie à la Cinématique et à la Dynamique   VII—Chronophotographie sur Plaque Mobile   VIII—Mouvements de l'Homme—Cinématique   IX—Mouvements de l'Homme—Dynamique   X—Locomotion de l'Homme au Point de Vue Artistique   XI—Locomotion des Quadrupèdes   XII—Locomotion Dans l'Eau   XIII—Locomotion Dans l'Air   XIV—Locomotion Dans l'Air   XV—Locomotion Comparée   XVI—Applications de la Chronophotographie   XVII—Chronophotographie Microscopique   XVIII—Synthèse des Mouvements Analysés par la Chronographie. In French.

Marey, E. J. *Movement.* 2139. Translated by Eric Pritchard. William Heinemann, London. 1895. [i]-[v], vi-xv, [xvi], [1], 2-323, [324]. 4¾ x 7½. Translator's Note, Preface, Contents, Index.

204 text figures (mainly from Marey's plates). Chapter I—Time II—Space III—Movement IV—Chronophotography on Fixed Plates V—Description of the Apparatus VI—Applications of Chronophotography to Mechanics VII—Chronophotography on Moving Plates VIII—Human Movements IX—Certain Movements in Man X—Locomotion in Man XI—Locomotion of Quadrupeds XII—Locomotion in Water XIII—Aerial Locomotion XIV—Aerial Locomotion XV—Comparative Locomotion XVI—Applications of Chronophotography to Experimental Physiology XVII—Microscopic Chronophotography XVIII—Synthetic Reconstruction of the Elements of an Analyzed Movement. This is a comprehensive account of Marey's investigations of movement using photography, which in some ways is more important then Muybridge's work.

Matuszewski, Boleslas. *Une Nouvelle Source de l'Histoire (Création d'un Dépot de Cinématographie Historique).* 1057. Softbound. No publisher, Paris. 1898. [1]-[5], 6-12. 4⅜ x 8. In French.

Mayer, J. P. *British Cinemas and Their Audiences.* 149. Dennis Dobson, London. 1948. [i]-[viii], 1-279, [280]. 5⅜ x 8½. This is an early sociological study of film preferences in terms of age, occupation and so forth. It is based on about 100 case studies.

Michaelis, Anthony R. *Research Films in Biology, Anthropology, Psychology, and Medicine.* 574. Academic Press, New York. 1955. [i]-[vi], vii-xvi, 1-490, [491]-[496]. 5⅞ x 9. This is an exhaustive textbook on the scientific uses of film.

The Modern Bioscope Operator. 621. Ganes, London. 1910. [i]-[xxi], [1], 2-159, [160]. 5¼ x 8¼. Advertisement, Publishers' Preface, Contents, Appendix [1] (Cinematograph Act), [2] (Home Office Regulations), [3] (Local Regulations), [4] (Act of 1751), [5] (The Children Act), [6] (Technical Tables), Index. 21 text drawings (mainly equipment). Chapter I—Introduction II—The Film III—The Optical System of the Bioscope IV—Limelight V—Electric Light VI—Types of Projectors VII—Manipulation VIII—Operating IX—Faults To Be Avoided. The information in this book is of historical interest.

Moffett, Cleveland. *Deeds of Daring Performed for the Cinema.* 2671. Softbound. Extracted from *The Strand Magazine*, no date (about 1915). 196-201. 6¼ x 9⅜. Four text photos, two of which are production stills. This is a short, popularly written article dealing with stunt men.

Morokhowetz, L., A. Samojloff, and A. Judin. *Die Chronophotographie.* 2531. Softbound. No publisher, Moskau. 1900. [i]-[ii], 1-27. 7⅛ x 10¾. Inhalt (on title page). Eight unnumbered pages containing 19 photos (mainly technical), and 20 text figures (mainly equipment). [Kapitel 1]—Die Chronophotographie (by Morokhowetz) [2]—Ueber die Wiedergabe der Inductionsströme Durch das Capillarelectrometer (by Samojloff) [3]—Graphische Darstellung der Vokale (by Samojloff) [4]—Ueber die Registrirung der Kurzdauernden Lichteffekte (by Judin). In German.

Muybridge, Eadweard. *Animal Locomotion: Prospectus and Catalogue of Plates.* 1076. Softbound. J. B. Lippincott Company, Philadelphia. 1887. [1]-[2], 3-18, [i], ii-xxxii. 5 x 7½. [Chapter 1]—Animal Locomotion [2]—Animal Locomotion Catalogue. This advertisement for the full-sized Muybridge plates contains important information about how and under what conditions the plates were made. The second section is especially valuable to the collector as it describes each of the 781 plates.

Muybridge, Eadweard. *Animals in Motion.* 1542. Chapman & Hall, London. 1899. [i]-[viii], ix-x, 1-264. 12 x 9½. Contents, Catalogue of Illustrations, Preface, Introduction, Prelude to Analyses, Appendix (Reprint of "Paces" Section of Newcastle's *Horsemanship*). Two unnumbered pages containing one photo, and 262 text photos (animals in motion). [Chapter 1]—The Walk [2]—The Amble [3]—The Trot [4]—The Rack [5]—The Canter [6]—The Gallop [7]—The Ricochet [8]—The Leap [9]—The Buck and Kick [10]—Change of Gait [11]—The Flight of Birds [12]—Records of Movement from Observation. The Preface to this book of plates includes Muybridge's version of the development of the zoopraxiscope. The plates in this book and those in *The Human Figure in Motion* are reprinted (on a much smaller scale) from Muybridge's huge *Animal Locomotion*.

Muybridge, Eadweard. *The Attitudes of Animals in Motion, Illustrated With the Zoopraxiscope.* 1043. Softbound. Extracted from *The Journal of the Royal Institution.* Royal Institution, London. 1882. 43-56. 5½ x 8¼. Seven text drawings. This is the paper read by Muybridge at one of the first presentations of projected, photographic motion pictures.

Muybridge, Eadweard. *Descriptive Zoopraxography.* 1688. University of Pennsylvania, Philadelphia. 1893. [i]-[iii], ii-xii, 1-44, 1-34, 1-14, [xiii]-[xiv]. 5 x 7¾. Some of the Subscribers to "Animal Locomotion", Preface, Introduction, Appendix A (Syllabus of a

Course on Zoopraxography), Appendix B (Advertisement for *Animal Locomotion*), Advertisement. Two unnumbered pages containing one photograph, and 54 text drawings. [Chapter 1]—Studio, Apparatus, and Method of Working [2]—The Walk [3]—The Amble [4]—The Trot [5]—The Rack [6]—The Canter [7]—The Gallop [8]—The Leap. This book contains the best technical description of Muybridge's work (Chapter 1 and Appendix A).

Muybridge, Eadweard. *The Human Figure in Motion.* 1541. Third Impression. Chapman & Hall, London. 1907. [i]-[vi], 5-277, [278]. 12 x 9½. Introductory, Catalogue of Illustrations, Appendix A (Facsimile Signatures of a Few of the Subscribers to *Animal Locomotion*). 435 photos. The introduction to this book of plates reprints a description of one of Muybridge's zoopraxiscope shows.

The National Film Archive. 1051. Softbound. National Film Archive, London. no date (about 1954). [1], 2-16. 6⅜ x 8⅛. This short booklet provides a good description of the major activities of the National Film Archive, a section of the British Film Institute.

National Film Library Catalogue: Part I, Silent News Films: 1895-1933. 1172. Softbound. The British Film Institute, London. 1951. [i]-[iii], iv-vi, 1-208. 5½ x 8½. Each entry in the chronological list includes title, date, catalogue number, description, distributor and length.

L'Office Français d'Edition. *Emile Reynaud.* 1499. Softbound. Cinémathèque Française, Paris. 1945. [1]-[2], 3-77. 5½ x 7¼. Les Débuts de la Cinématographie: Les Dessins Animés d'Emile Reynaud by Paul Reynaud, L'Oeuvre d'Emile Reynaud by Georges Sadoul (Five Inventions and Nine Films), Bibliographie by Georges Sadoul (52 books and articles), Table des Matières, Table des Illustrations. 29 text illustrations, nine of which are praxinoscope frames in color. [Chapitre 1]—Le Centenaire d'Emile Reynaud (by Georges Sadoul) [2]—La Vie d'Emile Reynaud (by Paul Reynaud) [3]—Texte du Brevet du "Théâtre-Optique" (by Emile Reynaud). In French.

Pepper, Dick L. *The Technique of the Photoplay.* 1794. No publisher, no place. no date (about 1912). [1]-[2], 3-254. 7 x 9⅝. This course in writing for the silent screen has practically no value today.

Pudovkin, V. I. *Film Acting.* 1074. Translated by Ivor Montagu. George Newnes, London. no date (about 1935). [1]-[4], 5-153, [154].

4¾ x 7¼. Written by the great Russian director, this is one of the very few books on film acting.

Pudovkin, V. I. *Film Technique.* 1097. Translated by Ivor Montagu. Enlarged Edition, Second Impression. George Newnes, London. 1935. [i]-[iv], v-xviii, 1-204. 4⅜ x 7. This is one of the half-dozen or so classic books on cinema technique.

Pudowkin, W. *Filmregie und Filmmanuskript.* 1112. Translated by Georg and Nadja Friedland. Lichtbildbühne, Berlin. 1928. [3]-[4], 5-251, [252]-[256]. 4¾ x 6½. Inhalts-Verzeichnis, Zum Geliet, Der Letzte Mann by Carl Meyer, Spione by Thea von Harbou, Der Katzensteg by L. Heilborn-Körbitz, Advertisement. *Das Filmmanuskript,* [Kapitel 1]—Was Bedeutet das Drehbuch? [2]—Der Aufbau des Manuskripts [3]—Einfachste Methode der Aufnahme [4]—Methoden der Bearbeitung des Materials *Der Filmregisseur,* [Kapitel 1]—Film und Theater [2]—Regisseur und Manuskript [3]—Regisseur und Darsteller [4]—Der Schauspieler im Bild [5]—Regisseur und Operateur *Filmkunst und Filmschnitt* by S. Timoschenko, [Kapitel 1]—Kinematographie und Film [2]—Die Montage des Films [3]—Grundsätze [4]—Montage [5]—Rythmus der Montage und Erforschung Ihrer Methoden [6]—Rhythmus und Höhepunkte [7]—Titel [8]—Schlusswort. In German.

Quigley, Martin. *Magic Shadows.* 1393. Georgetown University Press, Washington. 1948. [1]-[6], 7-191, [192]. 6 x 9. This popular history of the origins of the cinema is relatively complete, concise and easy to read.

Richter, Hans. *Filmgegner von Heute—Filmfreunde von Morgen.* 945. Hermann Reckendorf, Berlin. 1929. [1]-[4], 5-125, [126]-[128]. 7½ x 10. Vorwort, Anhang (List of 27 Films), Inhalt, Lesen Sie. 214 text photos, 200 of which are production stills. Four untitled chapters. In German.

The "Riley" Illustrated Catalogue. 1288. Riley Bros., Bradford. no date (about 1915). [i], ii-xvi, [1], 2-320. 6½ x 10½. Contents, Index. 648 text figures (mainly equipment). Section I—Introduction to the Optical Lantern:—Its Construction and Use II—Mechanical and Effect Slides III—Science Lanterns IV—Introduction to the Cinematograph. This early catalogue of projection equipment and accessories is especially valuable because almost every piece of equipment is illustrated.

Robson, E. W., and Robson, M. M. *The Film Answers Back.* 1401.

John Lane The Bodley Head, London. 1939. [1]-[6], 7-336. 5¼ x 8½. This book presents the optimistic view that movies have gotten better and better through time in response to audience demand.

Ronchi, Vasco. *Il Problema Tecnico del Cinema in Rilievo*. 2537. Softbound. Reprinted from *Atti Della Fondazione G. Ronchi*, Anno VIII, No. 3 (May-June 1953). Scuola Tipografica Calasanziana, Firenze. no date (about 1954). [1], 2-28. 6¾ x 9⅝. 14 text drawings (mainly technical). In Italian.

Rotha, Paul. *Celluloid: The Film To-Day*. 1085. Reissue. Longmans, Green and Co., London. 1933. [i]-[iv], v-xiii, [xiv]-[xvi], [1]-[2], 3-259, [260]. 4⅞ x 7½. The value of this book is that it brings together several reviews and essays by Rotha.

Rotha, Paul. *Documentary Film*. 1396. Faber and Faber, London. 1936. [1]-[4], 5-272. 5½ x 8¾. One of the classic books on documentary written by a film maker and critic, this work is valuable in a historical context. Many of Rotha's ideas are out of favor today.

Rotha, Paul. *The Film Till Now*. 2667. Jonathan Cape, London. 1930. [1]-[4], 5-363, [362]-[364]. 5⅝ x 8¾. Both Rotha's history and his theory are somewhat outdated. The value of this book lies in the production data in the appendix.

Rotha, Paul, and Griffith, Richard. *The Film Till Now*. 1390. Revised and enlarged edition. Vision Press, London. 1949. [1]-[6], 7-755, [756]. 5¼ x 8½. The first two parts of this book are almost exactly the same as when Rotha first published them (1930). The third section (by Griffith) tries to bring the history up to date. Unfortunately, Griffith could not realize the effect television was going to have on film any better than Rotha could realize the effect sound would have. The stills and production data (Appendix I) are the most valuable parts of this book.

Sadoul, Georges. *French Film*. 119. Falcon Press, London. 1953. [i]-[viii], 1-131, [132]. 7 x 9¾. This, like the other volumes of the National Cinema Series, is a good basic history up to the fifties. Like the other books in the series, there is no documentation.

Sadoul, Georges. *L'Invention du Cinéma: 1832-1897*. 142. Softbound. Editions Denoël, Paris. 1946. [i]-[iv], [1], 2-362, [363]-[364]. 5⅝ x 9. In French.

Sadoul, Georges. *Les Pionniers du Cinéma: 1897-1909*. 144. Softbound. Les Editions Denoël, Paris. 1947. [i]-[ii], [1]-[5], 6-626, [627]-[630]. 5⅝ x 9. In French.

A Descriptive Catalogue of the Filmic Items **121**
in the Gernsheim Collection

Schiffer, Aug. *Hoe Maak Ik Zelf een Familie-Bioscoop.* 1218. Softbound. Uitgevers-Maatschappij ,,Kosmos," Amsterdam. no date (about 1920). [1]-[4], 5-46, [47]-[56]. 5½ x 8. In Dutch.

Schliepmann, Hans. *Lichtspieltheater.* 247. Ernst Wasmuth, Berlin. 1914. [1]-[2], 3-104. 9¼ x 12½. In German.

Schmidt, Georg, Schmalenbach, Werner, and Bachlin, Peter. *The Film: Its Economic, Social, and Artistic Problems.* 447. Translated by Hugo Weber and Roger Manvell. Falcon Press, London. 1948. [i]-[iv], v-viii, [ix], 124 pages numbered 1-62 (facing pages numberd the same), [125], ix-xvi, [xvii]-[xviii]. 8⅛ x 11⅝. This book uses graphically set type and photos to reinforce the arguments in much the same way that McLuhan does today.

Scotland, John. *The Talkies.* 322. Crosby Lockwood and Son, London. 1930. [i]-[vi], vii-xv, [xvi], [1], 2-194, [195]-[196]. 4½ x 7¼. Except for the chapter on color, this is not one of the better early sound books.

Seldes, Gilbert. *The Movies Come from America.* 145. Charles Scribner's Sons, New York. 1937. [i]-[iv], v-viii, 1-120. 5⅜ x 8½. There is some good information in this book about the American film in the early 1930s. The spine of this volume carries the title, *Movies for the Millions.*

Simonet, Roger. *Cent Ans d'Image.* 1003. Softbound. Calmann-Lévy, Paris. 1947. [1]-[7], 8-287, [288]. 7⅜ x 9⅜. In French.

Smethurst, P. C. *Exposing Cine Film.* 341. Softbound. Link House Publications, London. no date (about 1936). [i]-[ii], [1]-[6], 7-71, [72], [i], ii-xv, [xvi]. 4¾ x 7. The early exposure meters in the advertisement are the most interesting aspect of this popularly written book.

Some Applications of Photography. 2530. Softbound. Extracted from *Discoveries and Inventions [of the Twentieth Century]* by [E. Creasey]. no date (probably 1914). 359-374. 5½ x 8⅜. This excerpt deals with the use of film in scientific motion studies.

Spencer, D. A., and Waley, H. D. *The Cinema To-Day.* 182. Oxford University Press, London. 1939. [1]-[9], 10-191, [192]. 5½ x 8½. This book is rather technical, and therefore, of course, way outdated. It emphasizes governmental production (G. P. O.) but includes sections on commercial and amateur filmmaking.

Stillman, J. D. B. *The Horse in Motion.* 1527. James R. Osgood and Company, Boston. 1882. [i]-[v], iv-viii, [9], 10-127, [128]-[129]. 9¼ x 12. Preface by Leland Stanford, Contents, List of Plates, Appendix (A Description of How the Photographs Were Taken). 214 unnumbered pages containing 107 figures, and 12 text drawings (mainly of horses in motion). Seven untitled chapters. This work is important because it is the first publication of Muybridge's work and one of the first instances of the use of photography to study motion.

Talbot, Frederick A. *Moving Pictures: How They Are Made and Worked.* 1849. William Heinemann, London. 1912. [i]-[vii], viii-xv, [xvi], [1], 2-340. 5⅜ x 8½. This book is concerned almost entirely with the technical aspects of the silent film.

Talbot, Frederick A. *Moving Pictures: How They Are Made and Worked.* 843. Entirely Revised Edition. William Heinemann, London. 1923. [i]-[vi], v-xiv, [1], 2-429, [430]. 5⅜ x 8½. The value of this book lies in the detailed descriptions and criticisms of the technical aspects of the silent film.

Talbot, Frederick A. *Practical Cinematography.* 1903. William Heinemann, London. 1913. [i]-[v], vi-xii, [1], 2-262. 4⅝ x 7¼. The major value of this book is the data presented about early scientific films and the suggestion (made in the last chapter) for a national laboratory set up like the Marey Institute in France.

Timoschenko, S. *Filmkunst und Filmschnitt.* 1112. See under: Pudowkin, W. *Filmregie und Filmmanuskript.*

Towers, Harry Alan, and Mitchell, Leslie. *The March of the Movies.* 2526. Sampson Low, Marston & Co., London. no date (about 1947). [i]-[iv], v-viii, 1-88. 7 x 9½. Contents, The Illustrations. 64 unnumbered pages containing 64 photos, 28 of which are production stills. Chapter I—We Present—"March of the Movies" II—Yesterday and Today III—Money, Money, Money (Rank) IV—The Script (Launder and Gilliat) V—Art for Pete's Sake (Sheriff) VI—Direction (Hitchcock) VII—Stardust (Kerr) VIII—The Camera (Neame) IX—Music (Mathieson) X—The Big Drum (Myers) XI—Here's Hollywood (De Mille) XII—Here's More of Hollywood (Sturges, Disney and Lloyd) XIII—The Audience. Some of the statements of the interviewees are of value, but the questions are, in general, very poor.

Trutat, Eug. *La Photographie Animée.* 1366. Softbound. Gauthier-Villars, Paris. 1899. [i]-[vii], vi-xii, 1-185, [186]-[190]. 6½ x 10. Préface by J. Marey, Avant-Propos, [Appendix] (Patents), Table des Matières, Advertisement. Two unnumbered pages containing two stills, and 146 text figures (mainly technical). Chapitre I—Origines de la Photographie Animée II—Applications Photographiques III—Manipulations Diverses et Manoeuvre des Appareils. In French.

Turpain, Albert. *Conférences Scientifiques.* 1184. Softbound. Cinquième Fascicule. Gauthier-Villars et Cie, Paris. 1924. [i]-[vii], vi-xii, 1-83, [84]. 5⅜ x 8⅜. In French.

United Nations Film Footage Library Index. 2538. Softbound. United Nations, New York. no date (about 1955). [i]-[ii], 1-61, [62]. 8⅜ x 10¾. Table of Contents. [Chapter 1]—Introduction [2]—Guide to Major Subject Headings for Each Country [3]—Subject Headings [4]—Personalities [5]—Meetings. The listings of footage available refers to a card catalogue in New York for a description of the film.

Waldekranz, Rune. *Swedish Cinema.* 1235. Translated by Steve Hopkins. Softbound. The Swedish Institute, Stockholm. 1959. [1]-[72]. 6¼ x 8. Film List (in chronological order, with production data for 79 films). 51 text photos, 47 of which are production stills. This popular history of the Swedish film is easy to read and informative. The stills and film list are of greatest value.

The Warwick Trading Co. Ltd. 993. Softbound. Warwick Trading Co., London. no date (about 1901). [1]-[3], 4-224. 6 x 9½. Contents of Catalogue (Index). 27 text photos and numerous drawings in the equipment section. This catalogue is divided into two sections. The first section lists apparatus and the second (57-222) lists films for sale.

Wells, H. G. *The King Who Was a King.* 1665. Ernest Benn, London. 1929. [1]-[4], 5-254. 4½ x 7¼. This is the description of a script with a great deal of interesting "editorial" suggestion. Some of these suggestions have become very popular (tail credits, for instance).

Wheeler, Leslie J. *Principles of Cinematography.* 2668. Third Edition, second printing. Fountain Press, London. 1965. [1]-[4], 5-424, [425]-[428]. 5⅜ x 8½. This well-illustrated technical book could be used as a text for professional filmmaking from camera work to the final lab print.

Winchester, Clarence, ed. *The World Film Encyclopedia.* 1826. Amalgamated Press, London. 1933. [1]-[2], 3-512. 5⅛ x 8½. This book contains a great deal of factual material, but the accuracy of some of it is questionable.

Wolf-Czapek, K. W. *Die Kinematographie.* 1383. Softbound. Union Deutsche, Dresden. 1908. [1]-[9], 10-120. 6 x 9. Inhalt, Vorwort. 41 text figures, four of which are production stills. I—Abschnitt—Die Physiologischen Grundlagen des Lebenden Bildes II—Die Photographischen Grundlagen des Lebenden Bildes III—Zur Geschichte der Kinematographie IV—Amateur-Kinematographie V—Die Aufnahme VI—Das Kopieren VII—Die Vorführung des Bildes VIII—Berufs-Kinematographie IX—Besondere Anwendungen des Lebenden Bildes. In German.

Wood, Leslie. *The Miracle of the Movies.* 1860. Burke Publishing Co., London. 1947. [1]-[12], 13-352. 5½ x 8½. The chief value of this book lies in its illustrations, many of which have been published very rarely.

Woolley, Edward Mott. *Cinema Thrills.* 2670. Softbound. Extracted from *The Strand Magazine,* no date (about 1917). 14 text figures, seven of which are production stills. This is a short description of how a dozen trick effects (driving through a brick wall, for instance) are produced.

Wright, Lewis. *Optical Projection.* 2212. Second Edition. Longmans, Green, and Co., London. 1891. [i]-[vii], vi-x, [1], 2-426, [427]-[428]. 4¾ x 7⅛. This magic lantern manual is more complete than most of the others in the Collection. It contains a large section on the use of the lantern in schools and for scientific demonstrations.

Zglinicki, Friedrich. *Der Weg des Films.* 2071. Rembrandt-Verlag, Berlin. 1956. [i]-[vi], 1-992. 6¾ x 9⅜. In German.

PART II

Bakewell, Frederick C. *Great Facts.* 1899. Houlston and Wright, London. 1859. Of filmic interest: The Magic Disc (97-101).

Bayley, R. Child. *Modern Magic Lanterns.* 1728. Second Edition. L. Upcott Gill, London. no date (about 1900). Of filmic interest: Advertisements ([i]-[xvi], Outside Back Cover) Chapter XIII—Moving Slides and Effects (80-84) Chapter XVI—Animated Lantern Pictures (102-106).

Brevets d'Invention Français: 1791-1902. 1045. Ministère de l'Industrie et du Commerce, Paris. 1958. Of filmic interest: Cinéma (287-301).

Catalogue de Musée Section L: Photographie Cinématographie. 2672. Conservatoire National des Arts et Métiers, Paris. 1949. Of filmic interest: Cinématographie (152-212).

Dyer, Frank Lewis, and Martin, Thomas Commerford. *Edison: His Life and Inventions.* 1646. Two volumes. Harper & Brothers, New York. 1910. Of filmic interest: Volume II, Chapter XXI—Motion Pictures (527-550).

Edison, Thomas A. *Mémoires et Observations.* 1458. Translated by Max Roth. Flammarion, Paris. 1948. Of filmic interest: Deuxième Partie—Le Cinéma et l'Art (27-55).

Fourtier, H. *La Pratique des Projections.* 329. Bound with three other books. Gauthier-Villars et Fils, Paris. 1893. Of filmic interest: Chapitre III, 34—Tableaux Mouvementés (38-41) 35—Tableaux Doubles (41-42) 36—Chromatropes (42-43) 37—Les Phénakisticopes (43-45) 38—Tableaux Mécaniques (45) 39—Tableaux Hydrauliques (45-46).

Frippet, E. *La Pratique de la Photographie Instantanée.* 1457. J. Fritsch, Paris. 1899. Of filmic interest: Chapitre XI—Applications de la Photographie Instantanée a l'Etude du Mouvement (191-213).

Gernsheim, Helmut. *The History of Photography.* 261. Oxford University Press, London. 1955. Of filmic interest: Students of the film must, of necessity, have an interest in the development of photography. Gernsheim's book is the best source for this information as it is only concerned with photography up to 1914. The areas of specific filmic interest are: Part I—The Prehistory of Photography (1-35) Chapter 30—The Photography of Movement (323-339).

Illustrated Guide to the George Eastman House of Photography. 508. George Eastman House, Rochester. 1954. Of filmic interest: Motion pictures (22) Cinematographe and Kinetoscope (23).

Käsemann, Erwin. *Das Raumbild.* 2539. No publisher, no place. no date (about 1946). Of filmic interest: [Kapitel] G—Wann Soll der Start des Raumfilmes Erfolgen? (12-13) H—Die Einführung des Raumfilmes in die Praxis (13-15) I—Die Patentlage Beim Zweibandverfahren (15-17).

Kircheri, Athanasii. *Ars Magna Lvcis et Vmbrae.* 420. Sumptibus Hermanni Scheus, Romae. 1646. Of filmic interest: Liber X, Pars III, Metamorphosis III—Per Specula Conuexa Cylindracea, & Conica (903-904, and Iconismus XXXIII, Figuram 4 (facing 901)) Liber X, Cryptologia Nova, Capvt II—De Speculis ad Steganographiam Catoptricam Necessarÿs (910, and Iconismus XXXIV, Figuram 1 (facing 913)) Liber X, Cryptologia Nova, Capvt IV—De Praxi Steganographica (912, and Iconismus XXXIV, Figuram 2 (facing 913).

Kircheri, Athanasii. *Ars Magna Lucis et Umbrae.* 414. Second edition. Joannem Janssonium ä Waesberge, Amstelodami. 1671. Of filmic interest: Liber X, Pars III, Problema III—Lucernam Artificiosam Construere (768) Problema IV—De Lucerna Magicae seu Thaumaturgae Constructione (768-770) Cryptologia Nova, Pars Prima—De Projectione Figurarum (789-794).

The Magic Lantern: How to Buy, and How to Use It. 1101. Houlston and Wright, London. 1866. Of filmic interest: [Chapter 17]—The Chromatrope (43-45) [19]—Revolving Figures (45-46) [20]—Moving Waters (46) Catalogue of Scientific Instruments —Chromatropes (12) Single Rack Slides (12) Changing Comic (13-15) Lever Slides (16-17).

The Magic Lantern: Its Construction and Use. 1100. Perken, Son, & Rayment, London. no date (about 1890). Of filmic interest: Chapter XI—Mechanical Slides (60-63) [Catalogue of Perken, Son, & Rayment]—Rackwork & Mechanical Slides (127-129).

Marey, E. J. *La Méthode Graphique.* 957. G. Masson, Paris. 1885. Of filmic interest: Cinquième Partie—Technique (427-652).

Marey, E. J. *Le Vol des Oiseaux.* 956. G. Masson, Paris. 1890. Of filmic interest: Chapitre IX—Analyse des Mouvements du Vol par la Photographie (128-147) Chapitre X—Succession des Mouvements du Vol Déterminée par la Photochronographie (148-166).

Minitography and Cinetography. 1242. City Sale & Exchange, London. 1939. Of filmic interest: Animals and the Cine Camera by John E. Saunders (90-93) The Cine-"Kodak" Special by W. Buckstone (29-32) The Personal Film by Gordon S. Malthouse (94-98) Cine Buyers' Guide (265-320).

Paris, John Ayrton. *Philosophy in Sport.* (Published anonymously). 2427. Three volumes. Longman, Rees, Orme, Brown, and Green, London. 1827. Of filmic interest: Volume III, Chapter I (1-27).

Patents for Inventions: Abridgments of Specifications 340,001-360,000. 548. Patent Office, London. 1932. Of filmic interest: The index (iii-ix) contains about two pages of listings for patents relating to film. The book covers the late 1920s and 1930.

Porta, Io. Baptista. *Magiae Natvralis.* 434. Christophori Plantini, Antverpiae. 1560. Of filmic interest: Liber III, Capvt II—(untitled description of the camera obscura) (94-97).

Résumé des Travaux Scientifiques de Mm. Auguste & Louis Lumière. 929. L'Union Photographique Industrielle, Paris. 1914. Of filmic interest: Première Partie, Chapitre Premier—La Cinématographe (9-28) Chapitre II—Le Photorama (29-37).

B. BOOKS NOT FOUND

Acres, Birt. *The Birtac for At-Home Animated Photography.*
Demeny, G. *La Chronophotographie.*
Plateau, J. *Sur la Persistance des Impressions de la Retine.*
Roget, Peter Mark. *Deception in the Appearance of the Spokes of a Wheel Seen Through Vertical Apertures.*

BOOKS BY THE GERNSHEIMS

Clive Bell and Helmut Gernsheim. *Twelfth Century Paintings at Hardham and Clayton*
Randolph Churchill and Helmut Gernsheim. *Churchill, His Life in Photographs*
Alison Gernsheim. *Fashion and Reality*
Helmut Gernsheim. *Beautiful London; Creative Photography; Focus on Architecture and Sculpture; Julia Margaret Cameron, Her Life and Photographic Work; Lewis Carroll—Photographer; The Man Behind the Camera; Masterpieces of Victorian Photography; New Photo Vision; The Recording Eye.*
Helmut and Alison Gernsheim. *Alvin Langdon Coburn, Photographer; A Concise History of Photography; Edward VII and Queen Alexandra; Historic Events: 1839-1939; The History of Photography; L. J. M. Daguerre; Queen Victoria; Roger Fenton; Those Impossible English.*

EXHIBITIONS FROM THE GERNSHEIM COLLECTION

The Museum of Modern Art, New York, 1950
Victoria and Albert Museum, London, 1951
George Eastman House, Rochester, 1951
City Art Museum, Bournemouth, 1951
Art Museum, Lucerne, 1952
Traveling Exhibits, 1952-1953, 1954, 1968-1969
Stratford House, London, 1953

Art Museum, Gothenburg, 1956
Fodor Museum, Amsterdam, 1957
Palazzo dell'Arte, Milan, 1957
Folkwang Museum, Essen, 1959
Wallraf-Richartz Museum, Cologne, 1959
City Art Gallery, Newcastle on Tyne, 1960
Bibliotheque Nationale, Paris, 1960
City Art Gallery, Frankfurt, 1960
City Museum, Munich, 1961
County Museum, Warwick, 1961
Wayne State University, Detroit, 1963
University Art Museum, Austin, 1967
Museum of Modern Art, New York, 1968
University Art Museum, Austin, 1968

Bibliography

Listed below are the published sources that were used in the preparation of this report that are not listed and described previously.

Ceram, C. W. (*pseud.* for Kurt Marek). *Archaeology of the Cinema*. Translated by Richard Winston. New York: Harcourt, Brace & World, n.d.

Gernsheim, Helmut, and Gernsheim, Alison. *Creative Photography: 1826 to the Present*. Detroit: Wayne State University Press, 1963.

"Helmut Gernsheim," *Camera* (English edition), XLVIII, No. 10 (October 1968), 48, 50-51, 53.

Notes

1. This is an abridged version of a Master's thesis (University of Texas at Austin) completed by Mr. Haynes in 1969. It is reprinted with his permission as the holder of the copyright. Mr. Haynes notes that the reader should be aware of the fact that the introduction has been left intact, although it was written in 1968-69 and is no longer entirely accurate. Moreover, since 1969 the Gernsheim Collection has been moved to new quarters and expanded.

2. Friedrich Zglinicki, *Der Weg des Films* (Berlin: Rembrandt-Verlag, 1956), pp. 9-114.

3. Martin Quigley, *Magic Shadows* (Washington: Georgetown University Press, 1948), pp. 13-84.

4. C. W. Ceram (*pseudo.* for Kurt Marek), *Archaeology of the Cinema*, trans. Richard Winston (New York: Harcourt, Brace & World, n.d.), pp. 13-20. This chapter discusses to some extent what other authors have done and (on p. 18) what Ceram's position is.

5. Helmut and Alison Gernsheim, *Creative Photography: 1826 to the Present* (Detroit: Wayne State University Press, 1963), p. 9.

6. The editors of *Camera* incorrectly give the date as 1915 ("Helmut Gernsheim," *Camera* (English edition), XLVIII, no. 10 (October, 1968), p. 48.

Volumes I and II of
Performing Arts Resources
will be indexed in Volume III.